CALL AUCTION TRADING

New Answers to Old Questions

CALL AUCTION TRADING

New Answers to Old Questions

edited by

Robert A. Schwartz
Zicklin School of Business, Baruch College, CUNY

John Aidan Byrne
Traders Magazine

Antoinette Colaninno
Zicklin School of Business, Baruch College, CUNY

KLUWER ACADEMIC PUBLISHERS
Boston / Dordrecht / London

Distributors for North, Central and South America:
Kluwer Academic Publishers
101 Philip Drive
Assinippi Park
Norwell, Massachusetts 02061 USA
Telephone (781) 871-6600
Fax (781) 681-9045
E-Mail <kluwer@wkap.com>
Distributors for all other countries:
Kluwer Academic Publishers Group
Post Office Box 17
3300 AH Dordrecht, THE NETHERLANDS
Tel: +31 (0) 78 657 60 00
Fax: +31 (0) 78 657 64 74

E-Mail <services@wkap.nl>

Electronic Services <http://www.wkap.nl>

Call auction trading: new answers to old questions / edited by; Robert A. Schwartz, John Aidan Byrne, Antoinette Colaninno
ISBN: 0-7923-7423-1

Printed on acid-free paper.
Printed in the United States of America

Contents

List of Participants

Douglas Atkin*	Partner	Efficient Frontiers

*At the time of the conference, Douglas Atkin was President & CEO of Instinet Corporation.

Kim Bang	President	Bloomberg Tradebook
Harold S. Bradley	Senior Vice President	American Century Investment Management
William Brodsky	Chairman & CEO	Chicago Board Options Exchange
William G. Christie	Dean	The Owen Graduate School of Management, Vanderbilt University
Kalman J. Cohen	Distinguished Bank Research Professor Emeritus	Fuqua School of Business, Duke University
Paul Davis	Senior Managing Director	TIAA-CREF Investment Management, LLC
J. D. Delafield	CEO	Delafield Hambrecht, Inc.
Marianne Demarchi*	Director of Strategic Marketing	Euronext

*At the time of the conference, Marianne Demarchi was with the ParisBourse. In September 2000, the Paris, Brussels and Amsterdam stock exchanges merged to create Euronext.

Ian Domowitz*	Managing Director	ITG Inc.

*At the time of the conference, Ian Domowitz was Smeal Professor of Finance at Pennsylvania State University.

Michael A. Dritz	Chairman	Dritz Enterprises, LLC
William Freund	Director, William C. Freund Center for the Study of Equity Markets	Lubin School of Business, Pace University
Allan Grody*	President	Financial InterGroup Holdings

*Allan Grody is also Adjunct Professor at New York University's Stern School of Business.

William Harts*	Executive Vice President, Corporate Strategy	The Nasdaq Stock Market, Inc.

*At the time of the conference, William Harts was Managing Director at Salomon Smith Barney.

Andrew Howieson*

*A At the time of the conference, Andrew Howieson was an official of Bond Connect, a fixed income system operated by State Street.

Peter Jenkins*	Managing Director	Deutsche Bank

*At the time of the conference, Peter Jenkins was with Scudder Investments. On April 8, 2002 Scudder was acquired by Deutsche Bank.

Raymond Killian Jr.	Chairman	Investment Technology Group, Inc.
Jan Kregel	High Level Expert	United Nations Conference on Trade and Development
David Krell	President & CEO	International Securities Exchange
William Lupien	Chairman	OptiMark, Inc.
Kai-Oliver Maurer	Head of Product Management Traders	Deutsche Börse
Russell Monahan	Director of Strategic Research	American Stock Exchange
Duncan Niederauer	Managing Director	Goldman Sachs, Inc.
Kenneth Pasternak*	Partner	Chestnut Ridge Capital

*At the time of the conference, Kenneth Pasternak was President & CEO of Knight Trading Group.

Junius Peake	Monfort Distinguished Professor of Finance	Monfort College of Business, University of Northern Colorado
Gerald Putnam	CEO	Archipelago, Inc.
James Ross	Senior Vice President, Global Strategic Business and Sales	Instinet Corporation
Robert A. Schwartz	Speiser Professor of Finance and University Distinguished Professor	Zicklin School of Business, Baruch College
Glen Shipway	CEO	Primex Trading
Cameron Smith	General Counsel	Island ECN
George Sofianos*	Vice President	Goldman Sachs, Inc.

*At the time of the conference, George Sofianos was Vice President, International and Research at the New York Stock Exchange.

Holly Stark	Principal and Director of Trading	Kern Capital Management
Benn Steil	André Meyer Senior Fellow	Council on Foreign Relations

	in International Economics	
Richard Tipaldi	Managing Director	Salomon Smith Barney
Daniel Weaver	Associate Professor of Finance	Baruch College, Zicklin School of Business
Bruce Weber	Director, Subotnick Financial Services Center	Baruch College, Zicklin School of Business
Robert Wood	Distinguished Professor of Finance	The University of Memphis
Susan Woodward*	Chairman	Sand Hill Econometrics

*At the time of the conference, Susan Woodward was on the senior management team at OffRoad Capital.

R. Steven Wunsch	President & CEO	AZX, Inc.

Conference Sponsors

Archipelago, Inc.
Bloomberg Tradebook
Chicago Board Options Exchange
Herzog, Heine, Geduld, Inc.
Instinet Corporation
Investment Technology Group, Inc.
Jefferies & Co.
Knight/Trimark Group, Inc.
The Nasdaq Stock Market, Inc.
New York Stock Exchange
OptiMark Technologies, Inc.
Security Traders Association
State Street Corporation
WR Hambrecht + Company

Preface

This book is based on the proceedings of *The Electronic Call Auction: New Answers to Old Questions*, a conference hosted by the Zicklin School of Business on May 16, 2000. The text includes the edited transcripts of the panel discussions and separate addresses by three major industry executives Douglas M. Atkin, formerly President and CEO, Instinet Corporation; Kenneth D. Pasternak, formerly President and CEO, Knight/Trimark Group, Inc., and William J. Brodsky, Chairman and CEO, Chicago Board Options Exchange.

The electronic call auction is an important trading vehicle in many market centers around the world, but is not well understood in the US. What are call auctions? How should they be designed and integrated with continuous trading in a hybrid market structure? As call auctions play a more central role in the US markets, how will they affect market quality in terms of transparency, order flow consolidation, and price discovery? These and other critical questions were asked at the conference while the efficiency of the US markets was broadly assessed.

This book, however, is not simply intended to be a historical record of the conference. We have edited the manuscript to make it more readable, understandable, and complete. Throughout, we have introduced new material obtained in follow-up interviews with many of the panelists. Our intention has been to flesh out the discussions and to keep the material as contemporary as possible without sacrificing the essential nature of the original debate. In addition, we have included an introductory chapter that has a simple description of a generic call auction. That chapter also discusses, in broad terms, the role a call auction could play in US equity markets.

As will be clear to the reader, some of the participants in the conference are very positive about call auctions, and others are not. One of the editors of this book, Schwartz, has, over the years, been a strong supporter of call auctions.[1] The opinions of the other two editors, Byrne and Colaninno, may best be described as neutral. However, we all agree on one thing: controversy can make for an exciting conference and a thought-provoking book. Our hope is that, when the dust eventually settles on this and other debates about the structure of our equity markets, our markets will be among the strongest and most resilient in the global arena.

All through the production process, we have worked with the panelists, and have taken pains not to put words in their mouths. Most important, they have all approved the final draft of the manuscript. We thank them for their assistance and patience. We also express our heartfelt thanks to the sponsors who made this conference possible (see page xi). In addition, a number of people have been helpful in the preparation of this manuscript. In particular, we thank Joe Marchese for his help in the preparation of the manuscript, and Avner Wolf, chairman of Baruch's Economics and Finance Department, for his constant support and encouragement.

Robert A. Schwartz

[1] It should be noted that, as an indication of his beliefs, Schwartz has been a consultant to and has held an equity position in AZX, the parent company of the Arizona Stock Exchange, which is an electronic call auction.

Introductory Remarks

About 12 months have passed since our last conference. In that short period, it is mind-boggling to think about all that has happened: from the introduction of decimalization to the demutualization of Nasdaq, from the removal of NYSE Rule 390 to the development of SuperMontage, from no ITS to a super NMS; from the ECNs to talk of a CLOB, it is a growing list, and it illustrates an important point. The markets, restless and responding to technological, economic and regulatory forces, are changing at a dynamic pace.

Today, there is something else out there I want to mention. It is a smaller cloud. In a metaphorical sense, clouds are good in this market because they bring liquidity. This smaller cloud, closer to the horizon, is moving toward center stage. It still has some way to come. This cloud is significant for us because it is emblematic of the electronic call auction, which is the topic of today's conference.

Our fundamental concern, as always, is with the big picture: trading costs, price discovery, volatility, consolidation, fragmentation and transparency. We have debated these issues without resolution for over a quarter of a century. The debate generally has been in the context of the continuous market. However, by approaching these issues from a different perspective, I hope that today we will find new answers to some old questions.

In 1995, I ran a call market conference at NYU's Stern School of Business. I was amazed at the response. One hundred and fifty people registered. Today, we are appreciably above that number. Many of the attendees in 1995 were from outside the US. Today, most of you are from the US. It is a tremendous turnout for a conference of this nature in the US Your attendance suggests how important the topic has become.

I first heard about call market trading in the late 1970s. Back then, just about nobody on this side of the Atlantic knew what the term meant. However, at the time, non-electronic call market trading was used in several European markets, including Paris, Brussels, Frankfurt and, further to the east, Tel Aviv. Over 100 years ago, the NYSE operated a call market.

Why are we now considering a trading venue that was replaced with continuous trading in a by-gone era? The answer is, we are not. We are not looking to bring back a dinosaur. The calls of the past were non-electronic. Many people miss this point. They say, "Bob, why do you want to go back to the way the NYSE was?" Let me be clear: today's conference is about a call that is computerized.

A traditional and a computerized call are two very different systems. Computer technology is essential for unleashing the power of a modern call. The call, in turn, makes excellent use of electronic technology. Before we turn to the electronic call auction, however, let us briefly consider the continuous market. We can do so in a simple way by looking at a transaction record. The record for a full day of trading in Pfizer is displayed in Figure 1.

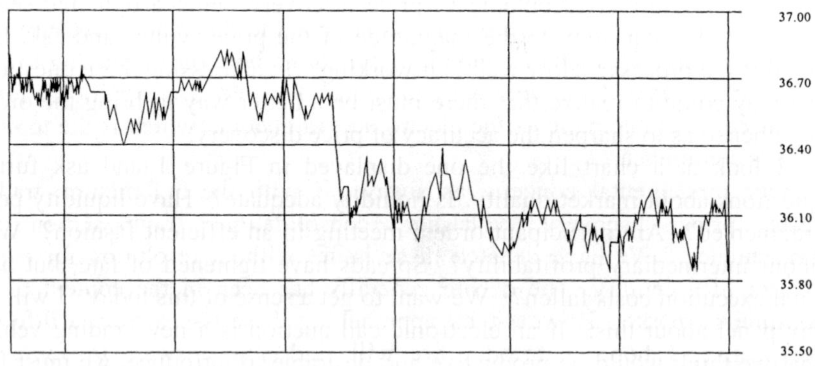

Figure 1. Full Day Price Chart for Pfizer, Inc., January 20, 2000. Source: www.stockpoint.com.

It is not difficult to find a transaction record that looks like this. Note the magnitude of the price swings. All sorts of stories could be told about what might have caused them. One is that information pertaining to Pfizer and/or to the broader market has changed. How convincing would such a story be? Does information release occur with sufficient frequency to account for the succession of rapid price movements displayed in the figure? Not very likely! Another story is that liquidity trading has also pushed the price around, having knocked it down when somebody's expenses had to be paid, or up when someone happened to have received funds. Could information trading and liquidity trading together account for the price changes displayed in Figure 1? I do not think so.

There is a third story that can be told. It is a story about price discovery – the enormous difficulty of finding prices that appropriately reflect the broad market's desire to hold shares. Some refer to such prices as "equilibrium values." I also like an equivalent term, "consensus values." Whatever the term used, finding these values is not a simple matter, particularly in an environment where participants differ in their individual assessments of share values. While each trader may know what he or she individually thinks Pfizer is worth, no one knows what everybody else is thinking. Consequently, consensus values are not knowable until orders arrive and transaction prices are established in the marketplace.

Look again at the Pfizer chart (see page xvi) and reflect on the intra-day volatility that it displays. There are a number of ways to quantify the intra-day price volatility, but one word sums it up: huge. To what extent is the intra-day volatility attributable to price discovery being a dynamic search process? We can look at the magnitude of the price swings and ask, how good is the process? How well is it working? In addressing these questions, we may come to realize that there must be a better way to bring the orders together so as to sharpen the accuracy of price discovery.

I look at a chart like the one displayed in Figure 1 and ask further questions about market quality. Is liquidity adequate? Have liquidity pools fragmented? Are participant orders meeting in an efficient fashion? What about intermediary profitability? Spreads have tightened of late, but have total execution costs fallen? We want to get a sense of this today. I will ask my panel about this. If an electronic call auction is a new trading vehicle that we think would be productive and desirable to introduce, we must first agree that our markets today need to be improved.

Sometimes, an innovation that is at heart simple can greatly increase the efficiency of an operation. To see this, let us consider an analogy.

Figure 2. Ye Old Checkout Corporation

Figure 2 represent a counter at a bank that is not fed from a common line. When you do not have a common line, you approach the counter asking, "Hey, what line should I get on?" You try to figure out how much business each person on each of the separate lines has to do, who the faster tellers are, and all that strategic sort of stuff.

Now look at Figure 3.

Figure 3. Orderly Checkout Corporation

Isn't this a nicer world to live in? We all appreciate the order brought by the simple structural change of getting everyone on a single line.

Back to the Pfizer chart.

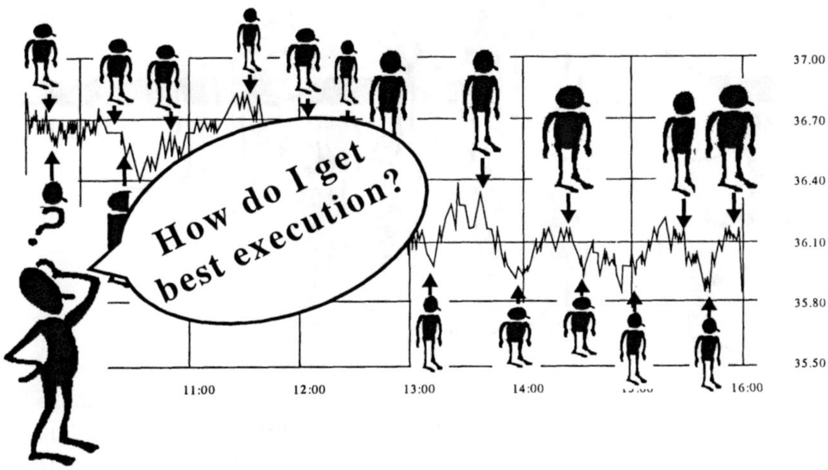

Figure 4. Did I Come in at the Right Time? (Full Day Price Chart for Pfizer, Inc., January 20, 2000. Source: www.stockpoint.com).

I want to sell, and you want to buy. When do I enter my order for Pfizer? When do you enter yours? How about others, when are their buy and sell orders entered? Figure 4 shows all those poor guys hanging around. There is one participant in the lower, left-hand corner, scratching his head and wondering, "When should I submit my order?" Is there something special that determines just when each trader enters his or her order? Is it the arrival of new information? Is it the occurrence of a liquidity event? Is it part of the search for best execution?

Figure 5 displays an alternative that is analogous to the "Orderly Checkout Corporation." In Figure 5, our participant has the opportunity to enter his or her order into a call auction and to transact in a multi-lateral, batched trading environment that gives all participants an execution at the same price. This environment is the topic of today's discussion. It is the call auction.

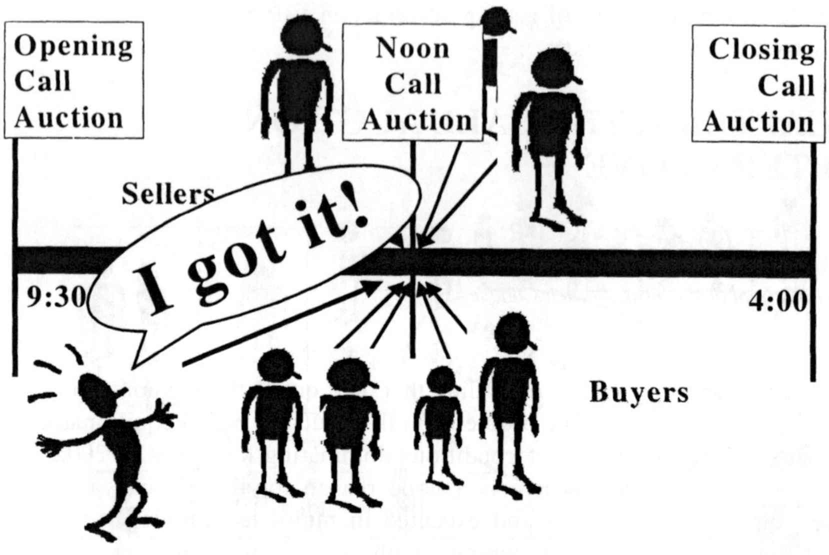

Figure 5. Order Entry into a Call Market

Those of you who know me may have sensed that I am supportive of call markets. But who knows what all the speakers and all of you in the room will say today? We have a distinguished group of speakers, and an equally distinguished audience. Many of you have your own strong positions. I am hoping to see some sparks fly.

Robert A. Schwartz

CHAPTER 1: THE CALL AUCTION ALTERNATIVE

Robert A. Schwartz
Zicklin School of Business, Baruch College

The call auction, a form of trading that died out in the pre-computer age, is making a comeback. The problems in the structure of US equity markets, worsened by the bear market conditions dominating headlines in 2002, are revitalizing the interest. There is a good reason for this. In call auctions, orders are batched together and executed in multilateral trades at specific points in time. That is in contrast with a continuous market where a transaction is made each time a buy or sell order meet in price. Recent advances in computer technology have considerably expanded the call auction's range of functions.

I suggest that the problems we are facing in the markets with liquidity, volatility and price discovery are largely endemic to the continuous market. I contend that call auction trading can counteract these destructive forces in the markets. In fact, the introduction of fully electronic call auction trading in the US would be the most important innovation in market structure. Indeed, the first market to fully introduce a call auction, be it the NYSE, Nasdaq, or an ECN or ATS, will, I believe, appreciably increase its ability to attract order flow.

There are countless design possibilities for a stock market. On a fundamental level, we have three generic structures: (1) the continuous agency/auction (order driven) market, (2) the continuous dealer (quote driven) market, and (3) the periodic call auction (which is also order driven).[2] Currently, much attention is focused on continuous, electronic

[2] The generics are typically not employed in their pure forms, however. For instance, agency/auction continuous markets commonly open with a call. The NYSE's order driven system includes intermediaries (the NYSE specialist, the floor traders, and upstairs market makers). A dealer can be included in a call auction (dealers, known as designated

limit order book markets (such as the ECNs). With a limit order book, public buyers and sellers can meet without the intervention of a dealer because the limit orders of some public participants establish the prices at which other public participants can trade by market order.[3]

An order driven platform may work well for retail order flow in liquid stocks under non-stressful conditions. But when markets come under stress, additional structural support is needed. The advent of more, and more rapidly disseminated news puts pressure on price discovery, as does the daily opening of the market. Market closes and the expiration of derivative contracts are generally stressful times. The arrival of a 100,000-share buy or sell order is stressful. Investors occasionally panic and prices go into free fall. In a bear market, the problems of maintaining a fair and orderly market are more apparent. Thus, the other two generics – market makers and the call auction – are essential for today's marketplace.

Dealers, specialists, and upstairs block positioners have historically been important providers of immediate liquidity in the US equity markets. The broker-dealers must be appropriately compensated. The bid-ask spread has traditionally been considered the source of their compensation. Broker-dealer operations, however, have borne the brunt of the extraordinary changes in recent years in our securities markets. When the dust has settled, will the services of broker-dealers be appropriately applied? Perhaps not. If our markets increasingly become disintermediated, the call auction will acquire enhanced importance. As a predetermined point-in-time meeting place, it enables the natural buyers and sellers to provide liquidity directly to each other.

---

sponsors, are included in both the call and continuous trading modalities in Deutsche Börse's Xetra). And so forth.

[3] The dynamics of the price process must, of course, compensate public traders for placing limit orders or else that market structure would not be viable. Research that I have undertaken with Puneet Handa suggests that limit order traders in a continuous market are compensated by a stock's transaction price mean reverting after the price impact of a liquidity event has caused a limit order to execute (with the mean reverting process implying accentuated volatility in the short run). The intuition behind the Handa-Schwartz model is the following. A limit order obtains an undesirable execution if the arriving market order that caused it to transact was motivated by informational change. However, liquidity events also trigger price changes and, if sufficient relative to the price changes caused by informational change, the liquidity driven changes can cause limit order trading to be profitable. This is because price reverts back to its previous level following an execution that was caused by an imbalance between liquidity motivated buy and sell orders. In the process, price volatility in short trading intervals is elevated. For further discussion, see P. Handa, R. Schwartz, and A. Tiwari, "The Ecology of an Order Driven Market," Journal of Portfolio Management, Winter 1998, pp. 47-55.

1. IT'S NOT A REVOLUTION, IT'S AN EARTHQUAKE

The equity markets in the US, and indeed around the world, are being reshaped by the simultaneous convergence of three powerful forces: technology developments, intensified competition (both domestic and global), and regulation. Each of the three may be individually viewed as desirable or well intentioned, but together their impact could produce results that are difficult to predict, hard to control, and not easy to understand. What we are witnessing does not resemble a revolution. It's an earthquake.

Over the years, we have witnessed the re-engineering of new financial products, the emergence of new investment styles, and the use of new quantitative trading techniques. Commissions have dropped sharply for many participants. Three decades ago, mutual funds, pension funds and other institutional investors were in their infancy; today they dominate the market. Nasdaq has become a powerful market center along with the New York Stock Exchange. And now, alternative trading systems (including the ECNs) are attracting significant order flow away from market centers.

Thirty years ago, daily price and volume data had to be manually collected. As a by-product of computer technology, we now have electronic transaction records for individual stocks. These records include all quotes, trades, and volumes, as well as times stamped in fractions of a second. The data have enabled users to see how execution costs can hurt portfolio performance. Investors, unsurprisingly, are seeking to control costs. From the individual's perspective, this can be pursued by the selection of a suitable broker as well as by careful order handling. Execution costs can also be controlled by suitable asset selection (illiquid stocks, for instance, might be avoided) and by market selection (illiquid marketplaces might be similarly avoided). But ultimately, the best way to reduce costs for all issuers and all investors is the creation of a better stock market.

Regulation has played a major role in market structure and efficiency. The involvement of the US Congress in market architecture started in the 1960s when it ordered the SEC to sponsor the Institutional Investor Study. The Report, which was filed with the SEC in 1971, focused largely on the competitive structure of the securities markets, the profitability of specialist operations, and the behavior of institutional investors. That is a group that was big enough even then to prompt the study.).

Next, in a sweeping overhaul of the Securities Exchange Act of 1934, Congress enacted the Securities Acts Amendments of 1975. The Amendments precluded the securities exchanges from imposing fixed commission rates and mandated the development of a National Market System (NMS). The motivations for the NMS mandate were, "the maintenance of stable and orderly markets," and, "the centralization of all buying and selling interest so that each investor will have the opportunity for the best possible execution of his order, regardless of where in the system it originates."[4] Still, best execution cannot be achieved without information, so this led the SEC to believe that the development of a central market system required that all price, volume, and quote information be available to all investors, for all securities and in all markets.[5] Recently, the SEC stated:[6]

One of the most important functions that the Commission can perform for retail investors is to ensure that they have access to the information they need to protect and further their own interests (page 7).

Although it intended to rely on competitive forces to the greatest extent possible to shape the National Market System, Congress also recognized that the Commission would need ample authority to achieve the goal of providing investors and broker-dealers with a central source of consolidated market information (page 33).

The consolidated, real-time stream of market information has been an essential element in the success of the US securities markets. It is the principal tool for enhancing the transparency of the buying and selling interest in a security, for addressing the fragmentation of buying and selling interest among different market centers, and for facilitating the best execution of customers' orders by their broker-dealers. Broad public access to consolidated market information was not the fortuitous result of private market forces, but of planning and concerted effort by Congress, the Commission, the SROs, and the securities industry as a whole (page 5).

However, a regulatory authority cannot become intimately involved with the production, distribution and pricing of market information without, at the same time, interfering with the natural formation of a marketplace. For this reason, despite the SEC's repeated statements that market structure should be determined by competition and not by the regulators, the Commission in recent years has become ever more deeply involved in the design of US

[4] See S. Rep. No. 94-75, 94th Cong., 1st Sess. 7 (1975) ("Senate Report"). For further discussion, see SEC Market Data Concept Release, Release No. 34-42208, December 9, 1999.

[5] See, for instance, Statement of the Securities and Exchange Commission on the Future Structure of the Securities Markets (February 2, 1972), 37 FR 5286. Also See SEC Market Data Concept Release, Op. Sit.

[6] SEC Market Data Concept Release, Op. Sit.

trading platforms. The effectiveness of this involvement has been questioned by a number of industry participants and academicians.[7]

In 1994, a paper by two professors, William Christie and Paul Schultz, published in *The Journal of Finance,* had far reaching consequences for the US equity markets in general, and for broker-dealer firms in particular.[8] Christie and Schultz had found that Nasdaq dealers were commonly avoiding odd-eighth quotes (e.g., 60 5/8). The authors suggested that dealers were "implicitly colluding" to keep spreads artificially wide. An investigation of the Nasdaq market and Nasdaq dealers by the US Department of Justice and the SEC ensued and a class action lawsuit was filed. Approval of the court was issued on November 9, 1998 of a settlement in the aggregate amount of $1,027 million.[9] Further, communications between broker-dealers about market conditions were also discouraged because the Department of Justice required that telephone conversations among traders be taped. This has made price discovery, particularly at market openings, considerably more difficult, according to many market participants

The SEC, continuing to press for greater transparency of price and quote information, in 1997 instituted new order handling rules. First, the commission required that any market maker holding a customer limit order must display that order in his or her quote. Second, the new rules stated that if a market maker has placed a more aggressively priced quote in an ECN, the market maker is in compliance if that ECN displays the top of its book in the Nasdaq quote montage. However, if that ECN's own best quotes are not in the quote montage, then the market maker must update his or her own quote in Nasdaq to match its ECN quote.

Continuing pressure from Washington has resulted in another important change. Between August 2000 (with eight NYSE stocks) through March 2001 (with the full set of Nasdaq stocks), the US markets changed from fractional pricing to decimals, with a one-cent minimum tick size. Although posted spreads have narrowed, depth at the best bid and offer has also declined. Liquidity is now distributed over many more price points while dealer spread revenues have dropped sharply.

[7] For further discussion, see, for instance, R. Schwartz and A. Colaninno eds., *Regulation of US Equity Markets,* Kluwer Academic Publishers, 2001.

[8] W. Christie and P. Schultz, "Why do Nasdaq Market Makers Avoid Odd-eighth Quotes?" *Journal of Finance* 49, 1994, pp. 1813-1840.

[9] Opinion by the Honorable Robert W. Sweet, 94Civ.3996, USD.C., Southern District of New York.

What have these changes accomplished for investors? Serious problems. Liquidity pools have fragmented, not consolidated. Intermediary profitability has been impaired for many market maker firms. Although spreads have tightened, it is not clear that total execution costs have fallen for institutional customers. Intra-day price volatility has been high. Price discovery is more difficult, especially at the market openings. Enormous price movements are commonly observed at initial public offerings. Are customers getting best execution?

A better trading system is clearly needed.

2. THE CALL AUCTION

An electronic call auction has been incorporated in recent years in a number of market centers around the world, most notably the ParisBourse[10], Deutsche Börse, and the London Stock Exchange. These electronic calls are not used as stand alone systems, but have been combined with continuous trading to create hybrid markets. That is because one size does not fit all. In a hybrid trading system, an investor can select among alternative trading venues based on the size of his or her order, the liquidity of the stock traded, and the investor's own motive for trading.

Three proprietary trading systems in the US have been based on call auction trading principles: Instinet's Crossing Network, Investment Technology Group's POSIT, and AZX's Arizona Stock Exchange. OptiMark (for equities) and State Street's Bond connect (for fixed income) are also call auction facilities.[11] Additionally, most electronic markets such as the Toronto Stock Exchange's Computer Assisted Trading System (CATS) and most floor-based markets, including the New York Stock Exchange, open trading with a call auction.[12]

[10] In September 2000, the Paris, Brussels and Amsterdam stock exchanges merged to create Euronext NV.

[11] AZX began operation in 1990. OptiMark Technologies and Bond Connect were both launched in 1999. All three systems are currently inactive.

[12] Peake, Mendelson, and Williams's proposed electronic system, which has been the prototype for most electronic continuous markets including Toronto's CATS, Paris's CAC, and Tokyo's CORES, incorporates a call as its opening procedure. See J. Peake, M. Mendelson, and R. T. Williams Jr., "The National Book System: An Electronically Assisted Auction Market," Proceedings of the National Market Advisory Board of the Securities and Exchange Commission, April 30, 1976.

Along with opening the market, calls could also be held twice during the trading day (e.g., at noon and at the close) or more frequently if desired (e.g., every hour).[13] The major equity markets in Europe (including London, Paris, Germany, Switzerland, Madrid and Stockholm) now use the call both to open and to close their markets. In the Far East, the Tokyo and Korea Stock Exchanges open and close both morning and afternoon sessions with call auction trading. The Taiwan and Kuala Lumpur Stock Exchanges go even further. They do not offer continuous trading at all. Instead, they run calls every several minutes for their stocks.

Over one hundred years ago, the New York Stock Exchange was run as a call market (non-electronic, of course). In some respects, the non-electronic call was a fine system for participants on the exchange floor, but it certainly had deficiencies for anybody away from the floor. Investors not physically present had little knowledge of what was happening (the calls offered no transparency), and access to trading was limited because shares of a stock could be exchanged only periodically (when the market for the stock was called). On May 8, 1869, the call procedure was abandoned when the NYSE merged with a competing exchange, The Open Board of Brokers, and became a continuous trading environment. The Tel Aviv Stock Exchange through the 1970s and the ParisBourse before the 1986 introduction of its electronic market, CAC,[14] also were non-electronic call auctions that did not survive. However, in recent years, tremendous advances in information technology and an array of other developments have created the conditions for the call's comeback.

Batching orders for simultaneous execution at a single moment in time is the essence of call auction trading. The principle of bringing orders together to determine a clearing price is discussed in more detail in the next section, *Order Batching in a Call Auction.* The clearing price in a call auction can be thought of as a "consensus value" because its determination is based on the full set of orders. While the discussion of Figure 1 (see page xvi) clarifies this and the principle behind call market trading, it is important to note that all call auctions are not alike.

[13] See Kalman J. Cohen and Robert A. Schwartz, "An Electronic Call Market: Its Design and Desirability," in *The Challenge of Information Technology for the Securities Markets: Liquidity, Volatility, and Global Trading,* Henry Lucas and Robert Schwartz Eds., 1989, pp. 15 - 58. Also see Nicholas Economides and Robert Schwartz, "Electronic Call Market Trading," with Nicholas Economides, *Journal of Portfolio Management*, Spring 1995, pp. 10 - 18.

[14] The acronym stands for "Cotation Assistée en Continu."

Economides and Schwartz identify four different auction designs.[15] (1) In a *price-scan auction*, an auctioneer announces tentative prices and traders state their buy/sell responses until the price that best balances the buy and sell orders is found.[16] (2) In a *sealed bid/ask auction*, traders submit priced orders that are not disclosed to one another.[17] (3) In a *crossing network*, traders submit orders that are matched at a price determined in some other market (i.e., trades are priced for the POSIT crosses using mid-spread values established in the major market center at the time of a cross). (4) In an *open order book auction*, traders follow the market until it is called as buy and sell quantities are cumulated and displayed at each price with a continuously updated indicated clearing price.

I first learned of call auction trading in the mid-1970s, just prior to participating in a conference in Israel. The talk I planned to give contained a discussion of bid-ask spreads. The Tel Aviv Stock Exchange, however, was using non-electronic call auction trading at the time, which meant that this part of my presentation had to be eliminated. There is no bid-ask spread in a call auction. It has, subsequently, become apparent to me that the differences between the call and continuous environments extend well beyond the bid-ask spread.

Call auctions, because they focus liquidity, have commonly been thought appropriate mainly for small cap, less frequently traded stocks. However, they also have particular appeal for the large caps because they cater to the needs of institutional participants whose portfolios are mostly comprised of these issues. Market impact is reduced for the institutional investor because the call is a point in time meeting place where orders are batched together for a multilateral trade Commissions may be lower in a call auction than in a continuous trading environment due to the greater ease of handling orders and clearing trades in the call auction environment. For the broad market, call auctions can reduce price volatility, unreliable pricing, unequal access to the market, and various forms of manipulation and abuse.[18]

One feature of call auction trading in particular deserves attention. The call auction is an explicit price discovery facility. That is, batching many orders together for simultaneous execution at a single price produces a consensus

[15] See Economides and Schwartz op. cit.

[16] For further discussion, see Cohen and Schwartz, op.cit.

[17] OptiMark was a sealed bid/ask auction. For further discussion, Eric Clemons and Bruce Weber, "The OptiMark Experience," in the *Electronic Call Auction: Market Mechanism and Trading: Building a Better Stock Market,* Robert Schwartz ed., Kluwer Academic Publishers, 2001.

[18] For further discussion of the properties of call auction trading, see Cohen and Schwartz, op. cit., and Economides and Schwartz, op. cit.

value that better reflects the broad market's desire to hold shares. Consequently, the call auction is a good opening facility for both the order driven (exchange) market and the quote driven (dealer) market. Moreover, because it is an explicit price discovery facility, call auction trading can be used to dampen intra-day price volatility.

3. ORDER BATCHING IN A CALL AUCTION

This section presents a simplified description of how participant buy and sell orders are sorted into two cumulative arrays that are matched against each other to determine the trades that are made. It also presents the single transaction price that is set in a call auction. We illustrate the principle of order batching in a call auction with reference to Figure 6. In each of the four diagrams share price is shown on the vertical axis. By simply letting all orders represent the same number of shares (e.g., one round lot), the number of orders at each price is shown on the horizontal axis.

The first diagram (Figure 6a) displays a set of buy and sell-orders. The orders are arrayed at each price based on the sequence in which they have arrived. The next three diagrams show how the orders are batched together to determine which execute, and the price at which they execute. Only the buy orders are shown in Figure 6b. At 51, the highest price at which any buy order has been placed, there is one order to buy. Two additional buy orders have been entered at 50 and thus, at 50, we have a cumulative total of three orders to buy. At yet lower prices, one order has been placed at each of the prices, 49, 48, and 47. Thus, the cumulative number of orders at these prices is four, five, and six, respectively.

Only the sell orders are shown in Figure 6c, and we can cumulate them much as we did the buys. The sell orders, however, are cumulated from the lowest price (48) up to the highest price (52).[19] The cumulative number of sell-orders increases by one order as we move from the single order at 48 to the five orders at 52. That is because there is only one sell order at each of the prices in this range.

The cumulative buy and sell orders are brought together in Figure 6d. The two curves intersect at the point were price is 50 and the number of orders is three. Thus, three buy orders (one placed at 51 and the two at 50)

[19] Buy orders are cumulated from the highest price to the lowest because the price limit on a buy is the highest price the trader is willing to pay (a lower price would gladly be accepted). Sell orders are cumulated from the lowest to the highest because the price limit on a sell is the lowest price the trader is willing to receive (a higher price would gladly be accepted).

are matched with three sell orders (one placed at 48, one at 49, and one at 50). At 50, the maximum number of shares trade. There is only one buy order at the higher price of 51, and only two sell orders at the lower price of 49.

Note that the most aggressively priced buy orders are matched with the most aggressively priced sell orders, and that three of the executed orders receive price improvement (the buy at 51, the sell at 49, and the sell at 48). The unexecuted orders are the buys at 49, 48, and 46, and the sells at 51 and 52. These less aggressively priced orders may be cancelled, rolled into the continuous market, or held for the next call, depending on the wishes of the trader.

4. WHY HAS THE CALL BEEN RESISTED?

If the call is such an excellent facility, why is it that electronic call auction trading has not been more widely used in recent years the United States? Two reasons are paramount. First, sell-side participants resist the innovation, fearing that it would dis-intermediate the market and, in so doing, hurt them economically. The second reason is ignorance.

The concern of the sell-side is understandable and hardly surprising. Broker-dealers, both on and off the floor, provide an array of services (information provision, order handling, transactional immediacy, account management, etc.) that help bring the customer to the market. However, because their compensation comes from commissions and the bid-ask spread and is trading related, technology that enables electronic trade execution and causes dealer dis-intermediation directly threatens broker-dealer revenues. To eliminate the problem, a minimum fee could be charged for all orders entered into the call. Broker-dealer firms would retain part of this fee as compensation for bringing the customers to the market. We note, however, that such an arrangement may conflict with the 1975 ban on fixed commissions.[20] Nonetheless, sell-side participants should recognize that any improvement in market structure would spur more growth of the aggregate order flow. Consequently, the pie that everyone shares would become bigger.

Ignorance is a formidable problem. On the surface, the call auction may seem like a simple alternative to continuous trading. When I first heard

[20] For further discussion, see Robert Schwartz, "Technology's Impact on the Equity Markets," in *Future Markets: How Information Technology Shapes Competition*, Chris Kemerer, editor, Kluwer Academic Publishers, 1998, pp. 137-152.

about it more than two decades ago, I viewed the call through the eyes of a micro-economist. I visualized orders being cumulated to form downward sloping buy curves and upward sloping sell curves that look like the demand and supply curves we teach our students in Economics 101 (look again at Figure 6d on page 14). The simple elegance of the price determination procedure is captivating, and I thought the call an innovation that could not be resisted. I have subsequently learned that far more is involved. The very subtlety of the procedure and the complexity of the issues it has implications for, have impeded the calls' acceptance. The issues include:

- Use of electronic technology in trading
- Structure of the call market
- Compensation of intermediaries
- Regulatory involvement in market structure development
- Buy-side traders' demand for immediacy
- Participants' order placement decisions
- Timing of information release
- Extended hours trading

Technology While information technology (IT) can be used to enhance continuous trading, it is essential for call auction trading. Moreover, the call auction is an extremely good environment for the application of IT.[21] In a continuous market, IT speeds up the rate at which orders can be submitted, displayed, and turned into trades. In so doing, it accentuates the importance of nano-seconds. In a call auction environment, on the other hand, IT is used to sort and cumulate orders and to find the clearing prices. It is apparent from a system such as AZX that, in a call auction environment, the computer is used to do one thing in particular that it was created to do – namely, to compute.

Call Auction Structure Considerable choice exists in call auction design. A poorly designed system will fail. Further, if a market center runs a call auction along with its continuous market, the two trading modalities must be properly interfaced. Achieving critical mass is a further problem. Much as a car cannot run without gas, a securities market will not operate without sufficient order flow. Even a well-designed call auction will fail if it does not succeed in its initial efforts to capture critical mass order flow.

[21] There is a tendency to use new technology to do better and faster what has been done in the past with an older technology (e.g., to mimic the procedures of continuous market, floor based systems), and non-electronic calls have been very inefficient. However, the successful introduction of electronic trading requires the design of new order handling procedures, and the call auction in an electronic environment becomes an excellent vehicle.

Dealer Compensation As discussed earlier, broker-dealers must be appropriately compensated when operating in a hybrid environment that has a dis-intermediated trading structure. In the short run, however, if the intermediaries do not accept that an innovation will improve market structure and benefit them financially, the innovation will be blocked. In the long run, the continued participation of the intermediaries in bringing customers to the market must be assured.

Regulatory Issues Commentators generally tend to focus on the spatial consolidation of orders, not on temporal consolidation, in considering regulatory issues on market structure. They also tend to focus on the size of the bid-ask spread and to ignore the accuracy of price discovery. Realigning the regulatory focus toward temporal consolidation and price discovery would facilitate the resolution of various regulatory issues. It could lead to market structure developing naturally rather than by regulatory edict.

Buy-Side Traders' Demand for Immediacy The conventional view is that buy-side traders demand immediacy. However, many institutional investors are more concerned about anonymity and keeping trading costs low than about obtaining immediate executions, per se. It is also widely believed that continuous markets provide immediacy. Nevertheless, large, institutional sized orders cannot, as a rule, be executed immediately at reasonable cost in our continuous markets. Ironically, for some customers, periodic call auctions could actually provide more immediacy than the continuous market.

Order Specification Limit and market orders have different properties in call auctions than in continuous markets. In a continuous market, limit orders placed on the book generally execute at their limit prices. In a call auction, limit orders execute at the common clearing prices, not at the prices at which they are written. In continuous trading, market orders are generally executed immediately at the counterpart market quote. In a call auction, market orders are held, along with limit orders, until the next call. At the next call, depending on the structure of the auction, market orders may be matched against contra-side market orders or treated as aggressively priced limit orders. Either way, the distinction between market and limit orders is minimal in call auction trading. Since limit orders and market orders have different properties in a call auction, participants should write their orders differently in this trading environment. Assuming no market impact, a buyer in a call auction should state the highest price he or she would be willing to pay. Similarly, a seller in a call auction should state the lowest price he or she would be willing to receive.[22]

[22] In the terminology of microeconomics, participants without market power should submit their reservation prices. Note that participants in a continuous market should never reveal

Information Release Information events are costly to limit order traders. Consequently, the prospect of news occurring discourages the placement of limit orders, thereby making markets less liquid. The release of some kinds of information is controllable (e.g., announcements of corporate earnings or unemployment statistics) while the release of other kinds is not (e.g., earthquakes or ice storms). With continuous trading, controllable information releases are commonly – but not all the time – made outside of regular trading hours. In call auction trading, controllable information releases that are timed in relation to the calls could be more readily made during the trading day. The more complex the information, the earlier it should be released before the start of a call. Having predetermined times at which the market will be called should facilitate the intra-day release of information without discouraging the placement of the limit orders that make a market more liquid.

Extended Hours Trading Prior to 1999, Instinet, a few other ATSs and the NYSE were offering after-hours markets to institutional customers. In 1999, under competitive pressures, the Big Board, Nasdaq, and others started to offer extended hours trading for retail customers. Yet the after hours market has remained relatively illiquid and volatile. Further, after hours trading blurs the meaning of a market's closing price. This can disrupt the various legal uses to which a closing price is put. For instance: the assessment of margin requirements in the cash market, marking-to-market in the derivatives market, and mutual fund purchases and redemptions. Call auction trading would certainly provide useful price discovery and liquidity provision to the after hours market. Further, call auction prices could be used for the various legal purposes just noted.

5. CONCLUSION

A call auction is potentially a powerful trading environment. Increasingly, it is becoming apparent that interfacing periodic call auctions and continuous trading modalities is a step in market structure development that must be taken. Over time, resistance to change and ignorance break down. It would certainly be desirable for our major equity markets to follow this approach to developing their hybrid structures.

These are among the issues that were discussed and debated at Baruch College's 2000 conference.

---

their reservation prices because doing so would result in the total elimination of the gains to trading.

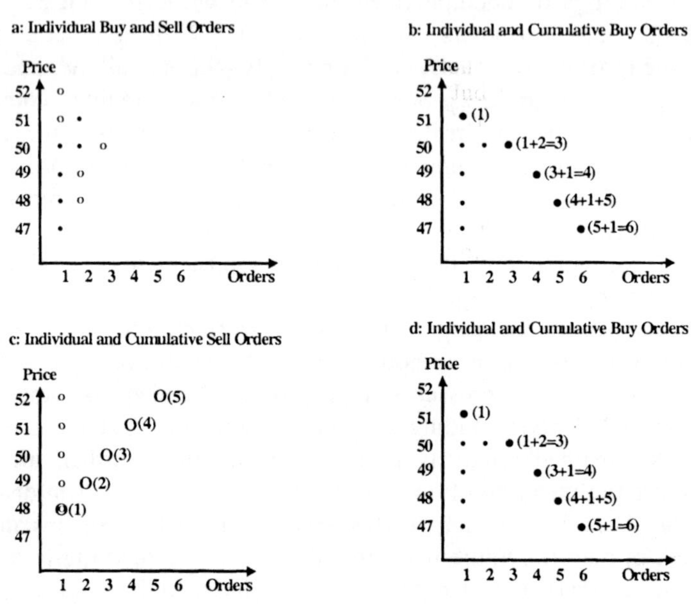

Legend:

- • Individual buy order
- ● Cumulative buy orders at the price or better
- o Individual sell order
- O Cumulative sell order at the price or better

Figure 6. Order Batching in Call Auction Trading

CHAPTER 2: THE BROAD PERSPECTIVE[23]

Moderator – Robert A. Schwartz, *Zicklin School of Busniness, Baruch College*
J.D. Delafield, *Delafield Hambrecht, Inc.*
William Harts, *The Nasdaq Stock Market, Inc.*[24]
Jan Kregel, *United Nations Conference on Trade and Development*
Marianne Demarchi, *Euronext*[25]
Duncan Niederauer, *Goldman Sachs*
Holly Stark, *Kern Capital Management*

ROBERT SCHWARTZ: To start, I would like to elicit all of your impressions about the quality of our markets today. Are they in good shape, bad shape, or what? Holly, you have a non-transparent look on your face. What do you think?

HOLLY STARK: As to your first question about the quality of markets, do we need improvement? Yes, I think so. It is pretty easy to answer it that way, but I won't go into a long explanation because I am sure you will ask other questions.

SCHWARTZ: What about you, J.D.?

J.D. DELAFIELD: I think there are problems with the quality of the market, both in its transparency and some of the processes.

SCHWARTZ: Let me put it this way. Fragmentation, to an extent, is in the eyes of the beholder. There are linkages between different liquidity pools and so, in one sense, the pools are not fragmented. But, in another

[23] This chapter is based on the transcript of the conference, The Electronic Call Auction: New Answers to Old Questions, held at Baruch College/CUNY on May 16, 2000.

[24] At the time of the conference, William Harts was Managing Director at Salomon Smith Barney.

[25] At the time of the conference, Marianne Demarchi was with the ParisBourse. In September 2000, the Paris, Brussels and Amsterdam stock exchanges merged to create Euronext.

sense they are, and the fragmentation we have is contributing to the difficulties of price discovery. Do you agree? Yes or no?

STARK: I do not think linkages work, Bob. That is the problem. There are linkages that ostensibly tie the markets together, but they are arcane and outmoded. The ITS[26] is one of them. We need to look at new linkages.

The ECNs are more forward thinking in that regard. They are building their own linkages. The ECNs do not have to go through the common switch that Nasdaq provides.

SCHWARTZ: What about price discovery? Who would like to respond? Has it become easier, better, crisper?

DELAFIELD: We should be circumspect about how we judge the quality of markets. I do not think that anyone would argue that there is not room for improvement. On the other hand, our securities markets in the United States today are probably more liquid and more transparent than they have ever been in history. Yes, price discovery is difficult, and it always has been. Call auctions in the case of the new issues market, which is where W. R. Hambrecht has its expertise, improve price discovery by bringing all buyers together at a single point in time to bid on a fixed amount of inventory. Because modified Dutch auctions[27] clear at the highest price that will sell all the inventory, no buyer can overpay (and, in fact, will probably pay less than he would have been willing to). Since everyone pays the same price, no one runs the risk of looking stupid at the end of the auction.

SCHWARTZ: What about volatility in today's market? Jan?

JAN KREGEL: There is no question that we have had an increase in volatility. The increase has come from a lack of linkages between alternate trading systems.

SCHWARTZ: I have not crunched out a set of statistics on it recently, but I do know that short-period volatility has always been accentuated. In the US equity market it looks very accentuated to me right now.

DUNCAN NIEDERAUER: The accentuated volatility may have something to do with changes in the composition of the volume. Something else we have observed is the recent growth of retail order flow and day trading.

[26] Intermarket Trading System (ITS) is a computer system that interconnects competing exchange markets. ITS is operated by the Securities Industry Automation Corporation (SIAC).

[27] In a classic Dutch auction between one seller and multiple, competing buyers, the auction starts at a high price and scans down until the first buyer steps forth and accepts the price. In contrast, in a classic English auction, the auction starts at a low price and scans up until only one buyer is left in the bidding.

SCHWARTZ: Good point.

NIEDERAUER: Think of how swiftly the pendulum has swung back in the direction of the retail investor. Think about the stocks being traded, about a lot of the new stocks that are being listed today, but that do not have a high percentage of shares that are actually floated. Think about what some of us have been calling the "CNBC phenomenon." Lots of people are watching CNBC, or are on Yahoo! Finance is in the news every day. New information is quickly disseminated to a far broader cross-section of investors than ever before. This is all contributing to levels of volatility that a lot of us have not previously experienced.

SCHWARTZ: It certainly is interesting how the rapid dissemination of information affects volatility. Does it cause problems in price discovery? Perhaps volatility over the longer intervals has not increased so much, compared with the accentuation of intra-day volatility. When volatility increases intra-day, but not on a daily or two-day basis, it means that a lot of intra-day overshooting is occurring. Prices go up too far, reverse direction, and then go down too far. To me, this is evidence of price discovery problems.

NIEDERAUER: The question is how are you going to uncouple price discovery from valuation? Historically, we have linked the two naturally. We assume that they are one and the same thing. In the pattern you just described, what is the root of the problem? If it's intra-day volatility, that suggests potential issues with price discovery.

Perhaps the more overriding factor is that a lot of people do not know how to value stocks anymore, and wonder about it when 20- or 30-point swings occur to a degree that we have never seen before.

SCHWARTZ: Price discovery and valuation are connected. What we like to teach in MBA programs is basic asset valuation, but those models do not go far enough. They have to be translated into how prices are set in real markets. In particular, we must recognize that, in the real world, different investors value stocks differently. How do we go from the array of individual investor evaluations to a single market evaluation that is to the price of a stock? It is a difficult step to take. Taking that step is what price discovery is all about.

Lets switch gears a bit. I would like to ask everybody a question. A little riddle, actually. The SEC had a recent release on market fragmentation,[28]

[28] Securities and Exchange Commission, Release No. 34-42450; File No. SR-NYSE-99-48, Self-Regulatory Organizations; Notice of Filing of Proposed Rule Change by the New York Stock Exchange, Inc. to Rescind Exchange Rule 390; Commission Request for Comment on Issues Relating to Market Fragmentation, February 23, 2000.

and the NYSE just came out with a report on market structure.[29] What do the two documents have in common?

STARK: They both addressed the issue of fragmentation, and also the need to have the greatest confluence of orders to achieve good price discovery. The New York Stock Exchange is concerned because, with the rescission of Rule 390, there could be more fragmentation. Certainly, the internalization of order flow in New York Stock Exchange stocks is a potential problem. The NYSE fears that internalization will hamper price discovery. The SEC's release discussed that specific issue as well.

SCHWARTZ: That is right Holly. But let me give you my answer. It is one that fits into the topic of today's conference. Both documents focus on the interaction of orders, on the pulling together of orders. They both care about consolidation. But neither of them thought of the time dimension of the problem. Both the NYSE and the SEC only focused on bringing orders together spatially, in a single market, or in linked markets.

What about bringing orders together at the same moment in time? Remember the Pfizer slide (see page xvi), and the question I raised about when should I enter my order? The inter-temporal aspect of fragmentation has received virtually no attention at all. The problem of the order flow fragmenting, fracturing over time has not been addressed.

Assume there is but one market. Let it be the NYSE or let it be Nasdaq. Regardless, if my order to buy arrives at 10:00 o'clock and your order to sell comes in at 10:05, how do our orders meet? In addition, traders are now breaking up their orders more and more, for submission to the market over more extended periods of time. I would like to turn to Holly with this one: If you are breaking up your orders and submitting them in smaller pieces over time, isn't that a form of fragmentation? Yes or no?

STARK: It is a form of fragmentation. If you look at block volume, there has indeed been a trend. Institutional traders are certainly breaking their orders up more than they used to. They are trading more over the course of the day. A lot of the institutions are doing so, trading throughout the day to get the volume-weighted average price (VWAP) for a stock.

It is the nature of the game. I have found in just the last few months that it is becoming harder and harder to get your arms around a stock and how it is trading. You can typically see a stock trading in a chunky manner, and you know there are institutions out there trading it. This is especially true for some of the more liquid Nasdaq stocks. But it is very rare to see prints of over 2,500 shares when there are thousands of trades. In many cases the

[29] Market Structure Report of the New York Stock Exchange Special Committee on Market Structure, Governance and Ownership, 2000.

trades are done on an automatic execution feature and executed through a wholesaler or whatever. It could be an institution that accounts for that volume.

Further, trading is being spread out over a longer day. You are trading before the market has opened and after it has closed. The after-hours market is really fragmented.

SCHWARTZ: Tell me, what difference does the following make? A: I am one trader and you are another trader. I send my order to market X on the Pacific Coast, and you send your order to market Y on the East Coast, and our two orders do not meet. B: We both go to the same market, but we each slice our orders into ten pieces and feed them in over time. What is the difference between A and B? Are the slices of my order able to meet and transact with the slices of your order? Aren't the two examples, A and B, equivalent examples of fragmentation? And, recognizing this, what role could a call play in this process?

DELAFIELD: The two examples are equivalent, and the call does have a role to play. A call auction should enable the order flow to be integrated properly, both geographically and over time. The call should enable the buyers who want to be owners of a security, rather than short-term traders of the security, to come out on top. If you know that, by virtue of receiving the security, you were among the people who were willing to pay the most for it, then you would never participate with the intention of flipping. This is because you would know that everyone out there who was willing to pay more got everything that they wanted. The caveat to this, of course, is that the marketing process must canvass the whole market.

SCHWARTZ: Jan, you have been involved in market microstructure for a long time. I know you have been interested in call markets. You have also been interested in technology more broadly. How do you see technology evolving, and how well do you see it being used?

KREGEL: When we look at the application of technology across a broad range of industries, we discover that new technology is almost always applied in a way that tries to mimic existing procedures. This almost always turns out to be the wrong approach. Look at new inventions. Their initial applications are typically to replace things that already exist. This is what is currently happening in the securities markets. New information technology is being used to mimic the way continuous markets trade securities. As a general rule, this is not the appropriate way to apply new technology. New inventions usually find their best applications by changing the ways in which things have been done in the past.

SCHWARTZ: What is the most appropriate way to use new technology?

KREGEL: I will answer this way. Volatility occurs when you allow different types of trading systems with different issues to exist. They should not be allowed to exist. The e-trading systems are an inappropriate use of the new technology because they also try to mimic something that exists – the continuous open outcry, rather than inventing something novel which, in the present context, is the electronic call.

Let me give you a simple example. Anybody who buys an airline ticket knows that it is virtually impossible to discover the price of an airline ticket at any point in time. I can call an airline company today and get a ticket price. But if I call another company or even the same company five minutes later and ask for the price of exactly the same trip, I will get a different price. The airlines are applying the new technology in the appropriate way in order to maximize their own interests.

SCHWARTZ: I should mention that Jan knows what he is talking about. He travels a lot. He just flew in from Geneva to be with us, and later today he is flying to Brazil. He has not yet decided where he will be at the end of the week.

KREGEL: But while it is in the interests of the company, it may not be in the interest of the buyer, because the new technology has decreased transparency and reduced each transaction to a bilateral exchange, or what we call a bilateral monopoly. Today, there is no such thing as perfect information in price.

Something similar appears to be happening in the securities markets. If Mr. A wants to trade a stock and Mr. B wants to trade the same stock, we set up a separate trading platform through an Internet connection to arrange a bilateral trade between Mr. A and Mr. B. But no one else has any knowledge of the trade or the price at which the trade is made. The more separate are the individual trading platforms, the more aggressive will be the competition amongst trading platforms for providing price improvement that nobody sees. But if nobody sees all the prices, then are they in effect there? And, will the potential benefit of those price improvements be realized?

When you have the NYSE, crossing systems, electronic communications networks, such as Island, competing aggressively for business, they are also competing in the application of the new technologies. As a result, this increases the probability of simultaneous transactions occurring at different prices because of the impossibility of price comparison and the implicit costs of having the different platforms.

SCHWARTZ: Continue on, Jan. Please expand further.

KREGEL: Those of you who are economists, know about some things called consumer surplus and producer surplus.[30] In standard

[30] The surplus that Kregel is referring to may be defined as follows: if all trades take place at the same price, buyers who would have been willing to pay more, and sellers who would have been willing to receive less, receive price improvement. The total surplus for buyers

microeconomics, you believe that those who would have been willing to pay more than the equilibrium price receive a consumer's surplus. It is the role of the monopolist to capture as much of the consumer's surplus as possible by differential pricing, thus maximizing his surplus in the form of monopoly profit.

Given a single market price, those who would have been willing to buy at a higher price receive a notional surplus and those who would have been willing to sell at a lower price also receive a surplus. But, if we break up every trade into a separate bilateral transaction engaged through an electronic medium, then all the surpluses disappear and some potential trades may not take place.

What alternative trading systems do, is they eat up the consumer surplus and the producer surplus. That, by definition, makes prices more fragmented, more volatile, and less efficient. It seems to me that this is what the new technology is doing with the multiple trading opportunities offered to individuals. Just as you no longer see a single airline price, I do not know what the price of Big Blue shares will be because I would have to scan different trading systems to find out what it is. I may not be able to do that. Similarly, I cannot say, "If I am going Phoenix today, I know what the price of the ticket is."

Clearly, the technology is being applied in a way that is not bringing out the kinds of price improvement that we would like to see in order to get more efficient pricing. On the Internet, this problem is solved by price scanning software, but the solution would not be available for securities trading. Furthermore, there is an alternative: the electronic call.

SCHWARTZ: So in the equities market, what should we do with technology? How do we solve our problems?

KREGEL: Bob has already mentioned that we should introduce electronic call markets. Call markets broke down originally because the technology was not there to allow them to function effectively. We now have the technology that will allow them to become efficient price discovery mechanisms. Why? Quite simply, call markets require everybody to meet at the same time. Physically, this is impossible, but with new technology, everybody can be together electronically. Everyone can be sitting at home and be present in the same market, at the same time, through a computer link-up. This solves the crowding problem.

It also solves the time dimension problem Bob was talking about. It allows the problem of random order flow, which created great difficulty under the old call market, to be resolved, because the orders can be bunched.

(and similarly for sellers) is the sum over all buyers of the price improvement per share times the number of shares trades.

That is, they can be brought together and batched together. The technology allows us to overcome the difficulties that existed under the old physical call market system, and it enables us get the orders price improved. In that way, buyers can realize their consumer surplus, and sellers can realize their producer surplus. By definition, this should be a win-win operation.

SCHWARTZ: There is one market that is making a lot more use of technology, and it is using the call auction far more than we are in the US. It is the market that was one of the original homes of the call market. It is the Paris Bourse.[31] Until the mid-1980s, the Paris market was a non-electronic call. I remember, one day, more than 20 years ago, when I was there, seeing it in operation. Somebody standing on a scaffold was writing down prices with a piece of chalk. Now the Paris stock market has an electronic call. Marianne, can you tell us why you came back to a call, and how you are using it?

MARIANNE DEMARCHI: Sure. The Paris Bourse has always relied on a call auction. As you mentioned, before 1986, we had this trading floor, and the traders would shout out the prices until an equilibrium value was finally discovered. In 1986, we implemented a new electronic trading system. It was an electronic order-driven market, and it was all continuous trading. Soon we realized that the continuous market was not appropriate for all types of securities, all types of trading strategies, or for all traders. Accordingly, we decided to implement additional trading mechanisms. Gradually, we have been implementing many different trading systems.

We currently make extensive use of the call auction – both to open the market and to close the market. We also use the call to trade small-cap, less liquid stocks. And we use it together with market making as a duel trading mechanism for what we call the high-growth company market.

We have introduced the call auction mechanism because we believe that it improves price discovery. It really helps liquidity, and it lowers the price impact of larger orders. It is a good vehicle for many types of trading strategies, and for encouraging the participation of retail customers.

SCHWARTZ: In Paris, you do not actually call it a "call auction," do you?

DEMARCHI: We call it a "fixing."

SCHWARTZ: In Germany, a call is referred to as an auction. I attended a conference a while ago in Germany, and was thinking, why do they keep talking about auctions? Why don't they say something about a call market? Then I realized that their term for a call market is an auction. So, it's an auction in Germany, and a fixing in Paris. The British always say things a

[31] In September 2000, the Paris, Brussels and Amsterdam stock exchanges merged to create Euronext.

little differently. In London, the call market is an uncrossing. This reflects the quote-driven heritage of the British market, and the dealer market use of the terms "locked market" and "crossed market" to describe, respectively, bid quotes that match offer quotes, and bids that are higher than offers. In a call auction, you want orders to lock and cross. When the orders cross, buys are above the sells, and the call clears them out through trading. That is, the call auction "uncrosses the market" at a well discovered price. We could have titled today's program "The Electronic Call Auction Fixing and Uncrossing Conference," but it did not look good on paper.

It is interesting, Marianne, that your continuous market, from its inception in 1986, has opened with an electronic call. I think you were the first of the electronic systems to also use the call to close your market. Were you the first? And why did you do it?

DEMARCHI: I believe we were the first. The main reason was that we observed high volatility during the last minutes of the trading sessions. I guess every market has this kind of pattern. It is really, really volatile before the close.[32] We concluded that a call auction would be a good way to gather all the people at this fixed point in time to lower this volatility, and to improve price efficiency. And it actually did.

SCHWARTZ: When you were considering putting in this closing call, was there any resistance, or was the innovation pretty widely accepted?

DEMARCHI: No, it was not widely accepted at first. Some investors and some traders were in favor, but others did not see the point and did not like the idea. The issuers, however, were in favor of the call auction. But we have always relied on a call auction. Consequently, we had this good feeling about the call auction, and so did the issuers. The issuers really did not like the elevated volatility at the market closings.

SCHWARTZ: It is interesting how much easier it is for me to interact with you, Marianne, and your colleagues in France, about a call auction. It is part of your history. Not too many of us were around 100 years ago to see the NYSE as a call auction. Moreover, the NYSE's call was an auction that did not survive.

I have another question, Marianne. Could you tell us how your closing call operates?

DEMARCHI: Technically, the market stops for five minutes at five p.m. For five minutes, all the open orders are gathered. There are no transactions. At 5:05, there is a confrontation of orders, a fixing.

SCHWARTZ: A confrontation of orders? A fixing?

DEMARCHI: Yes, well, the equilibrium price is discovered.

[32] "Volatility in US and European Equity Markets: An Assessment of Market Quality," Deniz Ozenbas, Robert A. Schwartz and Robert A. Wood, working paper, May 2002.

At the closing call, we see a totally different order flow than at the opening. There are many more large trades at the close than at the open. It is traders with large orders who are eager to trade, and they price their orders more aggressively. There are a lot of strategic orders that are placed in a type of reserve book. You do not like the term here, but we call them "hidden orders."

SCHWARTZ: I have no problem with hidden orders. Could you describe them a bit more for everybody?

DEMARCHI: They are an order type that allows you to show only part of an order. Hiding part of an order reduces market impact. Hidden orders are sometimes referred to as "iceberg" orders.

SCHWARTZ: We are also well acquainted with hidden orders. Many of our hidden orders, however, are hidden in the pockets of the floor traders. The trick is to get the orders out of the traders' pockets and into the trading mechanism.

DEMARCHI: Our closing call auction is an improvement in market quality. For instance, large volume trades that would take 20 minutes to execute in the continuous market, took only five minutes during this five-minute call period. At the same time, market impact is really low in the closing call.

SUSAN WOODWARD, Sand Hill Econometrics [From the Floor]: What fraction of the day's trading is done in the opening and closing call, compared with the regular session?

DEMARCHI: On average, the daily opening call used to be about six percent of total daily trading volume. It is now closer to three percent of the daily volume. The reason is that we open an hour earlier than before, and the participants need more time to receive and assess news. We do roughly four percent of daily volume at the closing call.

SUSAN WOODWARD [From the Floor]: Is this different for heavily traded stocks versus thinly traded stocks? Do the smaller companies on the Nouveau Marché market do a larger fraction of their trading in the calls?[33]

DEMARCHI: Yes, they do. When I say it is four percent in the closing and three percent in the opening quotes for the CAC Market, on the Nouveau Marché, it is the other way around. The call auction gathers a lot of volume -- roughly 60 percent of volume. But it is different. In the Nouveau Marché, the call auction largely attracts the retail trades, and the average

[33] The Nouveau Marché is a stock exchange designed to facilitate the contact between innovative high-growth companies and investors. It was launched on February 14, 1996, as an autonomous exchange operated, managed, and supervised by the Societe du Nouveau Marche (SNM), a 100% subsidiary of the Paris Stock Exchange.

trade size is low. The market making components of this dual trading system primarily attracts the really large institutional trades.

JUNIUS PEAKE, University of Northern Colorado [From the Floor]: I have two questions. First, what is your priority sequence for these trades? Is it price-time priority?[34]

SCHWARTZ: The answer is yes.

JUNIUS PEAKE [From the Floor]: Second, do you trade in decimals?

DEMARCHI: Yes.

JUNIUS PEAKE [From the Floor]: Good answers. One final question: Have you, Brussels and Amsterdam agreed yet on closing calls, opening calls and the rest of it, or is it too early to talk about this?[35]

DEMARCHI: It is a bit too early. There is a working group looking at the market model. We will probably use opening and closing calls, and we are also thinking about introducing intra-day call auctions.[36]

SCHWARTZ: On the intra-day call, let me point out that trading in Germany includes opening, noon and closing calls. I am currently working with data gathered from the Paris Bourse, and am interacting with Marianne on a study I am conducting with Mike Pagano from Villanova University.[37] Our findings suggest that price discovery at the close has been significantly improved by the introduction of the closing call. We also find that the introduction of the closing call has a positive spillover effect on the quality of price discovery at market openings.

A number of the European markets now have an auction at the opening and at the close. In the US, Nasdaq's Quality of Markets Committee has been considering opening the Nasdaq market with a single price auction. Some of us feel that this would be a meaningful step forward for price discovery, particularly in the thinly traded stocks in Nasdaq. So, why isn't there a single price auction mechanism for Nasdaq? Holly Stark and I are

[34] Price-time priority works as follows. First, the price of an order takes priority over time. For example, if a group of orders arrive, those that have the best prices receive priority execution. If all of those individual orders have the same price, each is executed on a "first come, first served" basis. As of January 2002, Nasdaq National Market Execution System (SuperSOES) uses price/time. See NASD Rule 4710 (1) (B).

[35] The Paris Stock Exchange merged in September 2000 with the Amsterdam and Brussels stock exchanges to form, Euronext.

[36] Euronext has a single trading platform and limit order book. Open and closing classes operate in this intra-day electronic continuous order-driven based system. Demarchi likens it to "an ECN" in the US

[37] That study is now completed. See Pagano and Schwartz, "A Closing Call's Impact on Market Quality at Euronext Paris," *Journal of Financial Economics,* forthcoming.

both on the Nasdaq subcommittee that is considering the issue. Would you like to comment on this Holly?

STARK: Your question is an excellent one. The subcommittee was formed to look at the opening prices of IPOs, as opposed to opening stocks in Nasdaq in general. There were also comments about how Nasdaq stocks opened vis-à-vis electronic orders coming in overnight, and about various dealers' opening moves at various prices. So a subcommittee was formed to look at the issues. Bob, as well as others from the buyside and the sellside, are part of the group. We have seen any number of permutations of electronic systems that could be used for a single price opening in Nasdaq. The thought right now is that perhaps Nasdaq's IPO problems will eventually spread to the rest of the market. The SEC in Washington has also pressured Nasdaq to open their market with a call. It would be a great step, but that step has not been taken yet.

JUNIUS PEAKE [From the Floor]: I want to break into the discussion here with a different question. Are we arguing for multiple markets here in the US that are all call-based? Or, are we arguing for a single call market where all orders come in? Do we want to put everything into the equivalent of a CLOB, a central limit order book, that is a call auction, so that the argument becomes one of a single-point of failure, a lack of competition? I am just suggesting that a consolidated call in one central place would be preferable to having several calls at the same time for the same security based on different order flows.[38]

SCHWARTZ: If it is helpful to give some context, I would be pleased to answer that, but I get uncomfortable at the thought that we are advocating something that everyone must do. Here is my context. I see the call as an alternative that would add to the efficiency of a marketplace. Our primary goal today is to understand how the call operates, and to assess its efficiency as a trading venue. As to where we might be heading with a call, I am very uncomfortable with anything that is mandatory. I personally am not suggesting that the call be turned into a CLOB.

STARK: I would hate to see the SEC or Congress come in and mandate something. I do not think we need more regulation. If someone comes up with a system that provides benefits for a lot of investors, if that system can naturally draw volume to it, then that system would become a de facto market center. But it should not stifle competition. I would really hate to see the SEC mandate anything.

Why are we having a conference on electronic call auctions? I think that a lot of people simply do not understand what a call auction is. A big

[38] Peake, in the above statement, is referring to a mandatory central limit order book, or so-called 'hard' CLOB. The alternative, a 'soft' CLOB, is not mandated by regulators.

educational process needs to take place before calls can truly be successful in the US

SCHWARTZ: Duncan, how do you think we should proceed with the educational process?

NIEDERAUER: We have spent some time with Steve Wunsch and his folks at the Arizona Stock Exchange (AZX). Starting on Monday, Goldman Sachs is going to launch a pilot centered around the Nasdaq opening. I think we have to walk before we run. We are optimistic that a solution will be figured out, and we are fairly agnostic about what the solution will be. We thought that by running a pilot, some of us might get some firsthand experience. Does this work? Or, are we spending too much time at these conferences talking about things that do not matter that much, and that cannot be improved upon that much?

With that spirit, we are going to start with just a handful of stocks next Monday. We are going to focus on the ten-minute period before the Nasdaq opening using the AZX platform. I think AZX is as good an open auction platform as there is out there. It also handles reserve orders, which I think is a good idea. What we heard earlier from Marianne is the key to a call auction. People must be able to hide prior to confronting each other and "fixing" price. We have to figure out a way to get reserve orders working with the other limit orders that are displayed. Let us take it for a test drive. Perhaps that will give the quality of markets committee an opportunity to see some of these things in action. We will try stocks of different shapes and sizes. We will try some of the liquid ones, find out where an opening call might be useful, and find out where it might not be useful, depending on a stock's underlying characteristics.

SCHWARTZ: I want to bring Bill Harts into this discussion. Bill, what do you think we will learn from the Goldman-AZX experiment?

WILLIAM HARTS: For the institutional representatives in the audience, I think you might see more liquidity than is typical for the Arizona Stock Exchange during that period in the next few weeks. It is great to sit here and talk about whether or not this would work. There is no substitute for real experience.[39]

[39] The experiment was not successful. There were some technical problems, such that some dealers were unable to get their automated position management system to work with the call. Those firms were not about to do these things by hand during the busy pre-opening hour, so that inability made the call a non-starter for those firms. It all amounted to a less-than-robust effort to get the auction going. In spite of some key supporters on the sellside, such as Duncan Niederauer of Goldman Sachs, and some philosophical supporters on the buyside, like Holly Stark of Kern Capital Management and Peter Jenkins of Scudder Kemper, in the end neither the dealers nor the institutions gave it more than token efforts. The experiment has underscored two major problems: 1) how difficult it is to get

Can I just mention one other thing? You brought it up before. It is the changing equity culture that we have in our country. Among all the great things that the Internet has brought to investing, one of the things that we look at is this sense of immediacy. The Internet empowers people to think that, "If I can have something right now, then it's good." Whether it is buying a book, or getting an airline ticket, or buying a stock, people expect it now. I am not sure how enthusiastic people would be if you told them that they had to wait an hour, or half an hour, or a minute, to buy a stock. I think we should take that into account when talking about the periodic call.

SCHWARTZ: Your point is very relevant for intra-day calls. But at the opening, unless people want to plunge ahead into the pre-hours market, they really are not waiting.

SUSAN WOODWARD [From the Floor]: On the other hand, E-Bay is one of the most profitable non-pornographic sites on the Internet.

SCHWARTZ: It is worth pointing out here that a call, is not a call, is not a call. Didn't Gertrude Stein once say this? A call can be structured in many different ways. We have had some poor calls in the past, and that always backfires. Because they were poorly structured, they do not work and, if they do not work, people turn around and say, "Hey, Bob why do you want to introduce a call?"

One of the key structural features of a call auction is the time of the day when it operates. AZX has not had an easy experience with that. The original time that AZX was allowed to hold its call was 5:00 pm. To be trading off-hours is, to say the least, not easy. It is not great to be running an operation when everybody is turning off their computers and going home to watch a Yankee's game.

HARTS: I want to mention something here that has not yet been said. The New York Stock Exchange has an electronic call auction at the opening.

SCHWARTZ: What makes it electronic, Bill?

HARTS: I think the orders come in electronically and are paired off electronically.

SCHWARTZ: There are degrees of electronic.

HARTS: However that may be, electronic or non-electronic, there is a pairing off of the orders at the NYSE open. Many of the orders come in electronically and are paired off. There has been no mention of this or evaluation of that fact.

---

something new going when it requires people to go out of their way to do it, and 2) how difficult it is when that new thing has a large critical mass hurdle, where you need a lot of people to make the switch simultaneously.

JUNIUS PEAKE [From the Floor]: Are you, Bob, in favor of having auctions at the same time that a continuous market operates, or are the calls in lieu of the continuous market?

SCHWARTZ: Jay, that is a big issue. How do you integrate call and continuous trading? The integration is not difficult at the open. The trading platforms in Canada, Europe, and the Far East are electronic, and they all open with a call. The call is an opening device. But the call is not only an opening device. It is a trading facility in its own right. However, when you introduce it at the close, there is an integration problem because the continuous market has already been running. One design decision is to halt trading for five minutes before the closing call is held. As Marianne has explained, this is the procedure in Paris. What if we have a call at noon? Could we have a call every hour on the hour? What do you think Marianne?

DEMARCHI: I do not know if a call every hour would add something positive to the market. I am not sure.

SCHWARTZ: Certainly, I could not imagine holding call auctions more frequently, because if you hold them too frequently you undermine the very purpose of the call.

DEMARCHI: That is what I meant. But to try the call more frequently would make sense.

SCHWARTZ: I would like to switch to a somewhat different focus. Something else has come up in our discussion that I would like to underscore the importance of. We have had 100 years of experience with continuous markets, and the call is a different creature. It is like going from Eastern riding to Western riding. With Eastern, you ride the horse one way. With Western, you ride it another way. People think that if you want to trade, you ride into a call auction the same way that you lope into a continuous market. Namely, that you put in the same order – price and size it in the same way. You shouldn't. There are a couple of other sport analogies. One involves snow skiing. We have downhill skis, cross-country skis, and snowboards. With each of these three different "vehicles," you operate differently. The orders entered into them should be priced and sized differently.

Nevertheless, some people have looked at how efficient the call might be for opening stocks by taking trades that have been made in the continuous market and inferring the orders that were behind the trades. They then ask, what if we batched these same orders together and opened the market with a call based on them? If you take a set of orders that were submitted into a continuous market with dealers, and alternatively match them using a call market algorithm, guess what would happen – all of the stocks will not open! Equivalently, I would like to see somebody who has spent his or her life on downhill skis set off on a snowboard using their old, downhill technique.

What happens? The skier falls, breaks a leg and says, "Who needs a snowboard"?

It is increasingly necessary to make call auctions work. If it is a good trading vehicle, we must actually bring it to fruition on this side of the Atlantic. To do so successfully, we need to be educated about it. In France, Germany, and elsewhere in Europe, people are accustomed to the calls. Their mental image of the vehicle does not have to be reset.

HARTS: I could not agree more. Within our own equity trading division, there are some traders who understand the concept of a call. These are mostly traders who have had experience with the New York Stock Exchange's opening. But as somebody has pointed out, to my surprise, a lot of over-the-counter traders are not familiar with it. Calls have never existed in the dealer market. They have never had occasion to use the call. So the education component is very important.

SCHWARTZ: Also institutions should know how to enter their orders differently. How would you see it, Holly, if you were to use a call?

STARK: I might actually put an order in on the opening. Right now, the majority of institutions do not enter any kind of order at the open. In the market, each dealer is opening his market at what could be a different price. So how do you know what the price really is? It is hard to get your arms around what your opening price is going to be.

SCHWARTZ: How would you price your orders? How would you price your buy if you were going into a call auction instead of a continuous market?

STARK: I think I would base it off of last night's close. I would also take account of any news that has come out, what the market looks like in the morning, what we are trying to get done in the course of the day, what our investment strategy is, and so forth.

SCHWARTZ: The dimension I am thinking of is, would you be more aggressive in your pricing?

STARK: Yes. I am sitting on a million-share order, and I know that I want to get 500,000 shares done during the course of the day because it is event-driven. But it is all part of strategizing your order.

SCHWARTZ: Would you be willing to put a higher price on a buy order, or a lower price on a sell order?

STARK: Sure. Very much, if I wanted to get a certain amount of stock in at a certain time. For various reasons, yes, I would do that.

SCHWARTZ: Would you price your limit order more aggressively in a call? In the terminology of the continuous market, would you be more apt to submit a "marketable limit order?" Of course, you do not know if your limit orders are marketable or not in a call until you know what the final clearing price is. A difference between the call and the continuous markets is that, if you put your buy limit order on the book of a continuous market, you will put it below the offer. Or, if you want to sell, you will state a limit price that is higher than the best bid on the market. You are waiting for the market to come to you.

STARK: You are providing an option for someone to trade off of the limit order that you have displayed to the market.

SCHWARTZ: If you put a limit order into the call, you can price it aggressively and wait for the market to form. Right?

STARK: Sure.

SCHWARTZ: You put in a buy order at 51 and the clearing price turns out to be 50. What do you buy at?

STARK: At 50. And I am very happy because I have gotten price improvement.

SCHWARTZ: You buy at 50 and you get price improvement.

GLENN SHIPWAY, Primex Trading [From the Floor]: I am responding to some of Holly's statements. This may all be academic, because in the coming weeks, OptiMark will go live for its 15-minute executions. OptiMark is a very sophisticated execution mechanism that effectively will produce a call every 15 minutes. Won't we find out soon enough whether or not calls work or do not work from the OptiMark experiment?

SCHWARTZ: What do all of you feel about Glen's question? Following up on what you were saying, Duncan, with regard to AZX, we will get more information. Is there anything more that one of you would like to add?

NIEDERAUER: Without passing judgment on the relative merits of OptiMark, I do not think that I would take the experience with any one system as validating or invalidating the entire concept of calls. It is a larger question. It is a question of how do we go from here to there. Maybe that will be discussed further on the panel that Junius Peake will be moderating later today. From the broker's perspective, we must listen to the people whom we talk to on the buyside trading desks. By extension, we also must listen to the portfolio managers, the planned sponsors, and the consultant community. These are the people who drive the process. They have to say that we really are going to get better executions in a call environment than we do in a continuous environment. That will be the deciding factor. When they make that decision.

SCHWARTZ: This discussion brings up something else that should be pointed out about any new trading systems. I have another analogy. Pick the car of your choice. Perhaps it is a beautiful, new sports car. What do you need for that sports car to run well? You need gas. I do not care what the car looks like, or how well the motor runs. With an empty tank, it will not go from zero to 60. It will stay at zero. It will simply sit in your driveway.

What is the equivalent source of fuel in a market? We can talk about market design up and down and all around, but just one factor, above all else, affects the quality of a market. What is it? It is whether or not that market receives order flow. Order flow is to a market, as gas is to a car. If you do not have it, you will have a beautiful car that simply sits in your driveway. So, how do we get from where we are to where we might like to go? Bill, I would like to ask you about the retail customers. Do you think that it is a field of dreams, that if we build it, they will come?

HARTS: This goes back to your point about education. It would require a giant leap to get the retail investors from where they are today to the concept of participating in a call. That is not to say that it cannot be done, or that it should not be done, but it will take time.

STARK: It will take time, I agree. If the retail customers understood that they would not be interacting just with other retail investors, but also with institutions, and with dealer principle bids and offers, they would be more attracted to the call. In fact, if the retail customers understood this, order flow would be attracted. But it is a chicken and egg problem.

SCHWARTZ: What is your experience with retail, Marianne?

DEMARCHI: What we see, at least with the opening call, is that there are a lot of retail orders. Most of the retail traders in Europe just call their brokers and say that they want their orders to be executed in the morning or in the evening. Usually it is in the morning. You do not have to explain that it is a different trading mechanism. It is simply a mechanism that gives price improvement, and price improvement helps different trading techniques and different traders.

Getting back to the institutional customers, we ran a survey of institutional investors and found that French institutional investors, depending on their trading size or investment objectives, do indeed need a different trading mechanism. The call would really fit most of their needs. Index traders, for example, want to trade at a price that they can benchmark on. They can use the closing price or the opening price for this purpose. They find it really useful to have a closing call. With a call, they are freer to price their orders aggressively when they are eager to trade. This is the point you were making, Bob, a few minutes ago, in your discussion with Holly. That is very good, not only for index traders, but also for patient traders and value managers as well. Instead of breaking up their orders, they just place them in a call.

SCHWARTZ: Holly, continuing with the institutions, a lot of the institutions go after the VWAP. Correct?

STARK: Yes.

SCHWARTZ: What if we have an alternative to trading at a VWAP price. Could the price set in a call auction environment be an alternative?

STARK: I do not mean to speak for every institution out there. But there are large mutual fund complexes whose traders are paid based on how well they beat the VWAP each day. Many are instructed to get the VWAP. Sometimes that is an easy way to trade. If you have a small order that you do not want to spend a lot of time on, and you have to get it done during the day, you just give it to someone and say: Please VWAP this.

However, VWAP can be dangerous. You may get the price, but if you did not get done what needed to be done, you have circumvented your investment process within your own firm. That is, it might be lovely that you completed 25,000 shares and that you got the VWAP or beat it, but you might be sitting on another 500,000 that you did not execute and perhaps should have. There are risks out there.

SCHWARTZ: Do you think you can get more volume done in calls? That is what you are suggesting, isn't it Marianne?

DEMARCHI: Yes. In our survey, it was found that abnormal volatility had disappeared in a call. The market impact was reduced. We discovered that the orders in the closing call were much larger; 50 percent larger than normal, and these orders were placed more aggressively than during the rest of the day. It is because of the concentration of orders on a call, the fact that it aggregates all of the orders for a period of time, and that investors are waiting for the call, that it makes it easier to place larger orders in the call.

STARK: I would think so also. The point Duncan made before is an excellent one. I am not sure a call is going to have that dramatic an impact on, say, Dell or Intel. But my firm trades small and micro-cap stocks, and it is my belief that, by concentrating volume a couple of times a day, you would get much more volume done. And the trades would be made at much fairer, and more equitable prices.

SCHWARTZ: A call is a meeting place that identifies two coordinates – time and place. Interestingly, by specifying the times of the "meeting points," more immediacy can be provided to the institutional customers than they currently receive from the continuous market. Thus, along with sharpening price discovery, calls should also get more volume done.

HARTS: Calls are a very good means of obtaining price discovery if you can ensure that the vast preponderance of trading interest is represented in the auction. Doing this may very well be impossible in a world where investors demand continuous trading. Anything short of critical mass in the call will cause the validity of the clearing price to be questioned.

JUNIUS PEAKE [From the Floor]: Calls also have the weakness of not aiding in the execution of options, since a person with an option may well want to close the trade immediately instead of waiting for one or more call times. In addition, a call market doesn't allow an almost immediate sale and replacement buy, since the sale must be completed before there are funds available to pay for the purchase.

STARK: I think a call is terrific for opening IPOs. IPOs are a nightmare right now, ever since the US Justice Department prevented market makers from talking to each other. Currently, it is very problematic to find a good opening price for an IPO.

SCHWARTZ: J.D., why don't you take it from there?

DELAFIELD: Anyone looking for the ultimate opening should be looking at the IPO market. It is probably the least transparent and most fractured market of all. Our firm has tried to introduce a call auction (as I said, we refer to it as a Dutch auction) into the pricing of initial offerings in the equity market.

Anyone who wants to see how we operate should watch tomorrow when our fourth deal, Nogatech is done using the Dutch auction process. It will be interesting to see in this market whether or not a lot of deals are coming, and whether or not the auction stands up better in difficult markets when prices are even harder to discover.

An interesting thing about the IPO market is that it is fragmented, but not because there are different marketplaces that are not talking to each other. It is fragmented because it is a subjective process. The dealers decide who to let into the market and who not to let in. Because of the economics of the business, they generally decide to let in only a few people. The rest of the market is invited in at the opening trade in the secondary, continuous market. This is why you see the great volatility in IPO trading on the first day. Generally, that volatility can last through the first few months after the deals have come.

We think this may be the most destructive kind of pricing you can have in the equity market. The result of a deal that trades up 200, 300, or even 400 percent on the first day is a massive hangover 90 days later. Ninety days later, most of the shareholders who own the stock are losers. Most of the people who have made money have moved on to better things, and most of the employees at the companies are unhappy. Furthermore, a lot of the new companies that are issuing a small amount of stock at a low price need to come back to the capital market for a follow-on offering. This time, the companies cannot find anyone to listen to their story because everyone who owns their stock owns it as a loser.

If you open the market up and let in everyone who wants to participate, you can discover price in a pre-public security. We do not think that the traditional arguments about retail running away with the deal are true. Retail customers are actually pretty rational, as are the institutions. To us, opening the market and running a call auction is a natural way to address the problem.

Obviously, the call auction is new, and the issues concerning its adoption are real. People do not flock to new systems readily. If a company chooses to have Goldman Sachs or Salomon take them out, it is a tough decision to change that and try something that is groundbreaking. How do you pull people away from something they are pretty confident will work because it has worked in the past?

Our Dutch auction will get successfully introduced in the IPO market when a few good companies decide to try it. I think you will see one of the major firms do that. In general, it is a better process. It brings transparency and, therefore, market quality. It reduces fragmentation. We have done three deals so far that have all been successfully completed. Two have traded well, one has not traded well.

SCHWARTZ: What effect do you see it having on price behavior after the opening? Will there be less of the run-up, less momentum?

DELAFIELD: With only three deals, it is hard to tell.

SCHWARTZ: What is your sense?

DELAFIELD: One tripled, one traded flat, and one traded up, then down, and is now down. I think they should trade up less. You are clearing out the people who are willing to pay more. The fear about using a Dutch auction to price an IPO is the winner's curse. Namely, you end up paying more than others are willing to pay. However, I emphasize that generally there are people who bid even more, and who nevertheless got the shares at the lower clearing price. This is because what we are running is a single price auction.

The more adoption there is, the more people will understand how it works. Bill Harts made this same point. But can you test-drive these things? I am not sure how well that works. You either adopt it or not. In theory, a Dutch auction should produce what Susan Woodward said – a boring market where the stock trades flat, and where you wait for some new market or corporate event to cause the stock to trade up or down.

SCHWARTZ: Let's take a couple of questions from the audience.

RUSSELL MONAHAN, American Stock Exchange [From the Floor]: I would like to ask J.D. Delafield who can participate in his auctions?

DELAFIELD: Anyone who is credit-worthy can sign the dealer's agreement and participate. I do not think you are going to find a portal or a neutral platform taking over because there is still the due diligence obligations and other services which companies and investors expect from the underwriters. So you are not just going to stick up a platform that says anyone who wants to sell stock, come list it here and we will gather up the orders.

RICHARD TIPALDI, Salomon Smith Barney [From the Floor]: I am curious about those three IPOs. The first one that had the high volatility, was it at the end stages? As you went down into the other three IPOs it was getting less and less close. I see the volatility in the IPO market being less and less because of the deals in general.

DELAFIELD: It is a good question. The real test will be tomorrow, when we see how Nogatech trades. Ravenswood was the first one, a $10 million deal a year ago (April 1999). It was a small deal that traded flat. It is really hard to draw conclusions from that. Salon.com was the second one, in July of 1999. It was a $28 million deal, and that one was very volatile. But I think the volatility was caused more by the part of the market it was in. It was the content space more than anything else. Andover.Net was an $82 million deal in December. It was a Linux company that had great volatility.

Salon and Andover, clearly, were very volatile, because of the markets they were in. In less frothy markets, we will see if we can go back to more of the Ravenswood type of trade: it was up five percent in the after-market, and stayed there until the next earnings release.

RICHARD TIPALDI [From the Floor]: Ravenswood wasn't as sexy as a dot-com?

DELAFIELD: It was a small deal, a small company.

SUSAN WOODWARD [From the Floor]: I tried to buy a piece of Andover through my own E*Trade account. When I got to the relevant trade page, I got a message that seemed to suggest that E*Trade was given only so many slots for bidders, that the slots were all gone, and that I could not bid. Do you still have an allocation mechanism for the cooperating broker/dealers, or was that some flaky thing specific to E*trade?

DELAFIELD: Without going into the quality of mind at E*Trade, they were not participating in the deal. I do not know why the message was posted there. They were not a dealer. If they had wanted to be a dealer, they could have been.

SUSAN WOODWARD [From the Floor]: With a broker/dealer who is cooperating with you, is it the case that any customer could have put in a bid, and that you would not have to restrict that broker/dealer to, let us say, only 5,000 customer bids?

DELAFIELD: The only restrictions are on ten percent orders, and any bid over one percent gets reviewed. We also do not allow any bids that are clearly thought to be manipulative. If someone bids $1,000 dollars a share, you have got to wonder: Are they trying to affect a market, or do they really want to own the thing at $1,000?

SCHWARTZ: Okay, we will continue to think about that. And as we integrate calls with the continuous, it raises the other question: Should we then change the design of the continuous market? Jan Kregel, can you give us a closing statement?

KREGEL: As long as we have got this competition within alternative trading platforms, I think we have got to expect increased volatility. Back to my airline analogy. Airline prices are a lot more volatile than they were before, and stock prices are, as well. We would do better to get to that "boring structure" that gives us a "boring market."

SUSAN WOODWARD [From the Floor]: The reason the airline prices are more volatile is because those trades are not printed. The only parties who see the price on those airline tickets are the buyer and the seller, which is why the airlines love it.

KREGEL: Exactly. That is the point. Fragmentation, lack of transparency, and price volatility all go together.

SCHWARTZ: J.D., what would you care to add?

DELAFIELD: The new issue market is just as relevant in the debate on call auctions as the exchanges. Whether it is the bond market, or the high-yield market, or whatever, you are seeing people apply this trading vehicle across the board. That also goes for private equity markets like what Off Road Capital is doing. We think that the call has great application, and that you will see more of it.

SCHWARTZ: Marianne, would you give us a closing comment?

DEMARCHI: Stock exchanges should try to respond to the different needs that various participants have in the market. That is not easy, of course.

SCHWARTZ: One size does not fit all. That is what we are finding, isn't it? The trick in market structure is combining the separate facilities into a well-structured hybrid. Bill Harts, what would you like to say?

HARTS: The talk about the VWAP reminds me of something that Ray Killian at ITG once said: VWAP is the strategy used when you dare to be mediocre. What VWAP really means is that no one on the buyside wants to be embarrassed by an execution. No one wants to buy at the high of the day, or to sell at the low of the day. They feel that by having a VWAP execution that will never happen. These people should be happy to enter their orders into a call auction.

For the call markets to be implemented in today's environment, much of the change must come from the buyside. We, on the sellside, spent a lot of money investing in systems that will hopefully lead to different alternatives in market structure. Now we would like to see the customer side say, okay, let us try using some of these new things.

SCHWARTZ: That would be great. Your thoughts, please?

NIEDERAUER: My thoughts are consistent with what Bill said. We go to a lot of committee meetings and conferences. It is clear to us that the things we are talking about, even though we do not think of them as sea changes, are viewed as such by many market participants. The participants see them as wholesale changes to the marketplace. You end up having to do a lot of these things and experimenting with many of them. As long as there is a lot of thought about doing something, one should go out for a test drive. Sometimes that is the only way we can find out.

It goes back to what you said before, about the wrong sports equipment for the wrong activity. There are lots of great ideas out there. But we have to put them out on the course and see how they go. That is the only way we will learn whether we took the right equipment out of the garage for the activities that our customers are trying to engage in.

None of us has all the answers. But it is incumbent on all of us, if we care about the markets, to address the question you opened with: can we improve the quality? If we did not think we could improve market quality, I do not believe that all of us would be sitting here today.

SCHWARTZ: That is true. I have heard some important people in the major market centers talk about the need to make big changes incrementally. Change should be made incrementally and voluntarily, so that we can see if it fits in as a natural property of the market. Your thoughts on that are interesting. Holly, you have the last word. Would you share it with us?

STARK: Changes are coming. Bill, your point is an interesting one. I was struck when you said before that there are people on your desk, sales traders, who do not know what a call market is. Unfortunately, a lot of people from the buyside still use the sales traders as their primary source of information on market structure rules. They might talk to these people 20, 30, or even 50 times a day. I find this very disturbing myself. I have tried to be an activist, tried to spread the word on lots of things, and call auctions have been one of them.

At the same time, there are lots of people on the buyside who understand how they have to operate in the markets on a day-to-day basis, and who realize that there are changes that need to be made. Buyside desks are making much greater investments in technology. They are interested in harnessing technology and in partnering or working with brokers who are doing creative things to get their executions done at cheaper prices, faster, and better. All of this is going to give the buyside an edge when they are ready to make those expenditures and embrace this new technology.

Ultimately, the changes are going to be profitable for us. But it will take some time. And education will have a big role to play.

SCHWARTZ: Thanks, Holly and thanks to all of you. It has been a very interesting discussion. We got lots of issues onto the table, and I hope that we will continue to build on them.

CHAPTER 3: VIEW FROM A MARKET MAKER[40]

Kenneth D. Pasternak
Chestnut Capital[41]

Today I hope to provide you a useful perspective on the electronic call auction from the point of view of a wholesale market maker. I think it is important to understand the history of Knight and our position on the market structure debate that is presently being waged. I will talk about issues relating to fragmentation, market transparency, and payment for order flow.

Knight is a market participant whose business model is premised on providing executions in continuous, dynamic markets. We provide liquidity—we guarantee immediate executions—during market hours to help ensure that retail-sized orders are executed immediately. Our vision of a "perfect market" at Knight is probably in sharp contrast to the proponents of a call auction. We advocate a continuous, 24-hour market in which individual investors can execute their orders immediately, at low cost and at the best price reasonably available at the time of execution. From an academic point of view, I suspect that there is an optimal market structure that would greatly improve market transparency, decrease volatility, eliminate intermediaries and seamlessly execute large numbers of orders instantaneously. However, in my opinion, if a proposed market structure is not able to satisfy the demands of the individual investor, then I regret to say that it has no chance of succeeding.

I have been in this business many years and have sat through countless presentations trying to sell me the better mousetrap. But I would suggest to you that any market innovation ignoring the basic premise—that a market center must satisfy customer demands—would stand no chance of success.

[40] This chapter is based on the transcript of the conference, The Electronic Call Auction: New Answers to Old Questions, held at Baruch College/CUNY on May 16, 2000.

[41] At the time of the conference, Kenneth Pasternak was President & CEO of Knight Trading Group.

Trading systems that attempt to repair market inefficiencies or weaknesses must do much more than that. They must also be able to compete with those market participants who have won market share through fierce competition. And I assure you that I have not met a market participant—an ECN, market maker, or exchange—that is unwilling to respond to competitive pressures.

We at Knight are in the business of providing that which the individual investor wants. That is what I have spent many years in my career constantly adapting to: Provide what the customer wants, or risk going out of business. Trust me, if the on-line investor demanded a call auction market structure and wanted his or her order matched twice or three times a day in a central location, then I guarantee you that my firm's logo would be "Knight: Where the Call Auction is Run."

When Knight was founded less than five years ago, the stock market had long been dominated by large, powerful institutional investors. We saw an opportunity to help restore balance by empowering, encouraging and serving the self-directed individual investor. Our goal is to provide the processing power for the on-line securities trading revolution by giving individual investors the same speed, low cost, and dependability in their securities transactions long enjoyed by institutional investors. And unlike traditional Wall Street market makers, we are committed to offering the same efficient, dependable service, whether people wish to trade a single share of a security or a thousand shares.

As you know, the popularity of on-line trading has surpassed all expectations, including ours. More than a third of individual investor transactions now occur over the Internet. Our company quickly became the leading destination for on-line trade executions. As a result, within three years of our founding, we were the largest market maker in Nasdaq and non-Nasdaq securities. In fact, in the first quarter of 2000 we handled almost 20 percent of dealer volume in Nasdaq and other over-the-counter securities. Numerous competitors have also thrived, and, like us, they have done so by recognizing the importance of self-directed individual investors and focusing on their needs.

The largest, most established Wall Street firms are primarily focused on serving institutions. They have long regarded retail customers as second-class citizens. Nevertheless, the self-empowered individual investor today is a driving force in the securities markets. Because our company and others are vigorously competing to serve these investors, they now command services and market access that were unimaginable at the time we founded our company.

1. THE SECURITIES MARKETS REVOLUTION

Let's suppose that today's date is May 16, 1995—instead of May 16, 2000—and that we are gathered here to debate market structure issues. And let's also suppose that I assert the following:

- First, over the next few years, millions of Americans will demand the ability to enter orders to buy and sell securities from their personal computers, twenty-four hours a day. And they will further demand the ability to trade from the beach or on the road, using small, wireless hand-held computers that fit into their pockets.
- Second, these same investors will insist on paying as little as five dollars per trade.
- Third, Americans will demand that their entire order, irrespective of quoted size, be executed and confirmed to them in a matter of seconds.
- Fourth, so many Americans will soon demand so much liquidity in the securities markets that trading volumes will be measured in *billions* of shares traded each day.
- And finally, to inform and facilitate their trading, individual investors will demand to receive real-time market information, delivered instantly to their homes and hand-held computers.

Had you heard these thoughts five years ago, no doubt you would have dismissed it as highly unlikely, even though all of these things have indeed come true. The securities markets *have* been transformed by the overwhelming popularity of on-line trading. Daily volumes in listed and over-the-counter trading *are* measured in billions of shares. And these things have come about because millions of Americans are seizing new opportunities to participate directly in the securities markets.

At the same time, they are demanding and receiving better and cheaper service to help them do it. For example:

Transaction costs for individual investors are at historic lows, with continuing downward pressure.

Market centers like Knight have invested millions of dollars in sophisticated technology to accelerate and increase the reliability of the execution process.

On-line brokers now provide individual investors with free or low-cost on-line research and market information that was simply unavailable to them a few years ago.

And perhaps most importantly, the market now provides even the smallest investor with instant liquidity at the best price available. At Knight Trading Group, we commit millions of dollars of our own capital every day, so that whether the investor wants to trade shares of Microsoft or an obscure over-the-counter issue, orders are executed in a matter of seconds, at low cost and at the best price available.

These dramatic enhancements in the marketplace have occurred not due to our company alone, but because of vigorous competition among many market centers pursuing the individual investor's business. In our eagerness to serve the self-directed investor, we and our competitors are continually lowering prices, committing capital, improving service and investing in new technology—all for the benefit of this newly empowered investor.

2. "DO NO HARM"

The secondary trading markets are instrumental to the capital formation process in this country as they allow large numbers of individual investors to share in the risks and benefit from the rewards of a vibrant economy. Indeed, I would argue that the ability of this country's securities markets to allocate capital efficiently among competing uses has greatly contributed to this country's unparalleled recent economic expansion. Therefore, the outcome of debates relating to market structure will have profound implications not just to the securities markets themselves, but also to this nation's economic future.

The existing market structure encourages vigorous competition among different market centers, each offering their customers a different value proposition. At Knight Trading Group, a large-scale market maker and processor of trades, our value proposition is to offer a combination of enhanced liquidity, speedy executions, price improvement, and dependability in trading 18,500 equity securities, as well as in trading options and equity indices. We enable our immediate customer—the on-line broker—to guarantee investors superior service, as well as low cost.

Is our company's trade execution service the very best available? For the typical self-directed investor, we certainly think so, but the marketplace will be the final judge. Only the marketplace can determine which company offers the superior value proposition for each type of investor.

There is no question, however, that robust competition in the marketplace is the best way to deliver optimal benefits for the investor. As Securities and Exchange Commission Chairman Arthur Levitt told the Economic Club of Washington last month, a market structure with multiple market centers competing with one another for business results in faster, cheaper and higher quality executions of customer orders.

3. WHY FRAGMENTATION IS A FALSE ISSUE

I can understand the concerns voiced by some market participants that the existence of multiple market centers creates isolated pools of investor orders, thereby reducing market efficiency. Let me explain, however, why these concerns about so-called market fragmentation are misplaced.

First, let's bare in mind an important principle that we have learned in recent years: Advancing technology batters down barriers and democratizes access to information. Technology has already produced dramatic improvements in market efficiency—and it will continue to do so.

Secondly, the securities industry's rapid consolidation in recent years has resulted in certain markets that are *less* fragmented than at any time in recent history. In the Nasdaq market, for instance, the top five market participants now account for approximately 60 percent of customer transactions compared with 40 percent ten years ago.

The mere fact that scores of electronic systems are seeking to become ECNs or ATSs does not signify a fragmented marketplace. As Chairman Greenspan recently stated: In the long run, unfettered competitive pressures will foster consolidation, as liquidity tends to centralize in the system providing the narrowest bid-offer spread at volume. To a significant extent, this consolidation already has occurred in Nasdaq.

I strongly suspect that those voicing the most concern about market fragmentation are really opposed to greater market competition. I also suspect that the call for "market reform" by some of these market participants is really a euphemism for "Let's turn back the clock": Let's turn it back to the days of $300 commissions, slow executions, inefficient technologies, and less competition to serve the interests of the individual investor.

To those who would return to that bygone era of charging investors fat commissions for the privilege of receiving indifferent service and minimal information, my response is this: The days of short-changing retail investors are over! It's time that we all compete just as hard as we can to empower and to serve the individual investor. It's time that we help individuals participate in the amazing benefits of our capital markets, so that they in turn can help deepen those markets and make them even stronger.

And to those who assume that best execution would be almost guaranteed in a centralized market, my response is this: Investors should not have to sacrifice the benefits of an innovative, dynamic marketplace merely to make the fiduciary's job a little easier. Investors are not only focused on the price at which an order is executed. In many cases, speed, enhanced liquidity and certainty of execution are also important priorities. To eliminate competition, to narrow the markets to a one-size-fits-all approach, would be to pander to the narrow interests of certain market participants, while denying investors many important options. Besides, in the end, one must ask: How good would even the best execution be in a marketplace devoid of real competition?

One final thought on the issue of market fragmentation: As one whose company has been built upon supporting market participation by individuals, I can tell you that individual investors who send in orders for 300, 400 or 500 shares now provide the market with so much liquidity that even the largest institutional investors are being forced to access that liquidity directly.

This is why the securities market paradigm is shifting. The market centers processing the order flow from self-directed individual investors are increasingly those providing the highest quality price discovery and the greatest liquidity. The individual investor increasingly controls market prices, not the institutional investor or the institutional brokerage firms.

The issue, then, is not that the marketplace has become more fragmented; it has not. The issue is that liquidity patterns are changing and creating a more level playing field for individual investors. The reason we are having this debate about market structure is that these changing liquidity patterns have eroded the advantage long enjoyed by institutional investors and by the large Wall Street brokerage firms that cater to them.

This change is healthy, and it is no reason to stifle competition. In fact, the changes in the marketplace demonstrate that our existing regulatory framework is working and will continue to deliver impressive, tangible results for all investors—individuals and institutions alike.

4. MARKET TRANSPARENCY

Now, let me address two other issues: market transparency and payment for order flow. Again, let me remind you of another time-tested principle: The regulation of US securities markets—arguably the most enlightened in the world—has always rested on the precept of full and fair disclosure. That is, by providing all investors—not just market professionals—with clear, adequate information, we empower them to make intelligent choices among all the available options without unnecessarily stifling competition or innovation.

SEC Chairman Levitt has called for a voluntary private sector initiative to make limit order books available to the public, while Commissioner Laura Unger recommends that all market centers be required to provide uniform information on various best execution factors. Both of these recommendations would improve market transparency, and both should be adopted. Better-informed investors are more likely to participate in the capital formation process, making our securities markets even deeper and more liquid in the process.

There is no justification for the age-old practice of market professionals walling off access to important market information. It is neither fair to individual investors, nor healthy for the marketplace. All investors should be provided not only with quotation and trade information, but also with the limit order files of the various market centers and with information that objectively measures the quality of execution at those market centers.

Chairman Levitt's recent call for a voluntary private sector initiative to improve the transparency of limit order books across all markets is vital to ensuring that investors receive the benefits of intermarket competition. Knight Trading Group wants to ensure that limit order information becomes available to the individual investor, and we look forward to working with the SEC and other securities market participants to that end.

Commissioner Unger's suggestion is equally important. If investors themselves had the information to identify which market centers have superior execution standards and trading protocols, their orders inevitably would receive better execution. At Knight Trading Group, we have begun publishing our execution standards and protocol on our website. We will soon begin publishing execution results as well—including price improvement rates, enhanced liquidity rates, immediacy rates, and price disimprovement rates—and we encourage all of our competitors to do the same.

5. PAYMENT FOR ORDER FLOW

Next, let's turn to the practice of payment for order flow. It has been the subject of incessant debate because it obviously poses a potential conflict: If a market center like ours gives brokers cash rebates or other inducements, how can the investor be sure that an order will receive the best possible execution?

Incidentally, I find myself in the strange position of defending a practice that costs our company an enormous amount of money. In 1999, we rebated nearly $139 million to our broker-dealer clients who sent us their order flow. What our client firms did with that money is a question best answered by them, but no doubt they would tell you that, because of those rebates, their customers paid lower commissions, received more free real-time market data, and more free technical and fundamental analysis of securities.

Let's begin by acknowledging that the securities industry is rife with conflicts. Besides payment for order flow, why not debate the wisdom of combining the broker and dealer functions in one company; or of allowing securities firms to both underwrite securities and issue research reports on them? After all, the most conspicuous conflict on Wall Street is that broker-dealers habitually recommend the purchase of securities for which they also make markets, or for which they provide banking services. Once again, the solution to such conflicts is not to disallow them, which would do severe damage to the efficiency of our capital markets. Rather, it is to insist upon full and fair disclosure.

Payment for order flow should be approached in a similar light. Indeed, the SEC debated the issue in the early nineties and concluded that full and fair disclosure was the right approach. By giving investors high-quality, real-time market information and execution results, by providing them with a clear explanation of each market center's policies, procedures, execution standards and trading protocols, and by fully disclosing any practice that might be considered a conflict of interest, we empower them to make intelligent choices among all of the available options.

The cash rebates paid by our firm have important benefits for the investor. They give us the volume of order flow we need to guarantee fast, dependable order execution at the best available price in over 18,500 securities. Outlawing the practice would eliminate investor access to immediate liquidity for any securities they wish to trade. Rather than denying investors this access simply because of a potential conflict, it would be far better to ensure that they have the information and the tools they need to detect evidence of inferior service.

There is strong evidence that cash rebates are not adversely affecting firms' order routing decisions. For instance, many firms that do <u>not</u> accept cash rebates route their customer orders to Knight and receive the same quality executions as firms that do accept cash rebates. The real power that brokers possess is not the ability to demand cash rebates, but rather, to demand higher quality executions for their customers. On-line brokers are able to assert the power of many with the voice of one. Knight's clients constantly look to us to find innovative ways to improve the quality of our executions for their customers. This competitive pressure has resulted in guarantees that would have been unheard of a few years ago, such as guaranteed automated price improvement, guaranteed executions greater than the quoted size in a matter of seconds, and mid-point pricing at the opening of the market and IPOs.

Let me also point out that cash rebates are not the only form of inducement for order flow. To truly understand this issue, one also needs to examine reciprocal order-routing and clearing arrangements; soft dollars; directed brokerage; and commission recapture programs, where institutions and their advisers receive rebates in the form of cash, research or brokerage services in direct relation to the amount of order flow sent to a broker-dealer.

The accepted broker-dealer practice of executing orders internally poses the same potential conflict. How can investors be assured that each order will be executed quickly and fairly when the broker is, in effect, trading against them?

In each case, the solution to perceived conflicts lies in full and fair disclosure. Again, we would welcome an opportunity to help improve industry standards and practices.

6. CONCLUSION

As we enter the second half of 2000, we are on the brink of dramatic regulatory and market structure changes that will forever change how we trade. Furthermore, we are only at the beginning stages of a stock market revolution that empowers individual investors, encourages them to participate in our capital markets system, and challenges Knight and our competitors to serve them better. If investors demand markets to be open 24 hours a day, seven days per week, then competition will meet the demand.

A Utopian might envision a securities market completely free of intermediaries and transaction costs, one that also provides unlimited liquidity and exhaustive market information. This market may be a twice-daily call auction or a centralized black box. However, the market structure that will prevail must be able to constantly satiate the rising demands of the American investor—and my prediction is that a model based upon continuous, instant liquidity will prevail.

CHAPTER 4: ALTERNATIVE CALL AUCTION DESIGNS[42]

Ian Domowitz, *ITG, Inc.*[43]
Andrew Howieson[44]
Raymond Killian Jr., *Investment Technology Group*
William Lupien, *OptiMark, Inc.*
James Ross, *Instinet Corporation*
Bruce Weber, *Zicklin School of Business, Baruch College*
Susan Woodward, *Sand Hill Econometrics*[45]

IAN DOMOWITZ: I am not the biggest fan of call auctions. Nevertheless, preparation for this panel has led me to think through some questions about the call auction, and about the importance of some assumptions that underlie various market mechanisms. Optimality in the context of a call mechanism usually means perfect information – everyone knows everything – and a frictionless market.

Proponents of call auctions cite their optimality. That theoretical position is not valid in my opinion. On the other hand, there are probably some interesting ways in which call auctions could be used to respond to various market structure issues. Let us start with the evolution of the simplest possible call market mechanism – the crossing function. To do so, I will

[42] This chapter is based on the transcript of the conference, The Electronic Call Auction: New Answers to Old Questions, held at Baruch College/CUNY on May 16, 2000.

[43] At the time of the conference, Ian Domowitz was Smeal Professor of Finance at Pennsylvania State University.

[44] At the time of the conference, Andrew Howieson was an official of Bond Connect, a fixed income system operated by State Street. Bond Connect is now inactive.

[45] At the time of the conference, Susan Woodward was on the senior management team at OffRoad Capital.

turn first to Ray Killian, one of the architects of organized institutional crossing. Ray, will you say some words about crossing, especially about the design of a crossing facility?

RAYMOND KILLIAN: I am glad to hear you define POSIT as a crossing system. We do not have any price discovery function in the call market that we run. We call it a point-in-time call. We run these calls seven times a day.

There is quite a bit of liquidity in POSIT. The system has evolved over the past twelve years with support from a lot of institutions that are present in this room today. Over the years, POSIT, in a sense, has merged with the continuous auction markets. Today, connectivity allows people in the aggressively active, price discovery auction market, to move their orders into a crossing session that is pricing off of the primary market. These people use sophisticated trade auto-management systems. We will see more of this in the future as connectivity improves.

The fragmentation issues that we discuss are real, but they are largely mitigated by new technology. As trade auto-management systems become more sophisticated, people can move their orders from the ECNs or some other alternative trading system, into the crossing systems, and from there into the auction markets. It will become easier to move back and forth among these alternative venues.

I am not convinced that we are about to see very complex price discovery call auctions play a major part in the intra-day market previously described this morning. I see the logic of it for the opening and closing rotations, but simple price discovery (probably between the bid-offer spread with defaults to the mid-point) makes more sense given the hyperactivity that we see today.

There is a great deal of mistrust among institutional investors placing orders in the open market. This is because prices are being displayed, offered, and discovered at the edge. To a large extent, it is the retail customers who are posting the bids and offers. If we had a montage on Nasdaq and on the NYSE that showed two or three price levels up and down, there would be more confidence in what is available, and at what size. Not knowing the orders that are available is contributing to the volatility that we are currently seeing.[46]

[46] SuperMontage is a voluntary system that displays the total amount of trading interest in Nasdaq at the "best bid" price and at the "best offer" price, as well as two trading increments away from those prices. The system also offers auto-execution capabilities for market makers while offering electronic communications networks and unlisted trading privileges the choice of auto-execution or order delivery. It also offers market makers and ECNs a variety of order types and a choice of execution parameters.

The success of our crossing system has been helped by information leakage in the institutional marketplace. The crossing system keeps confidential the identity of the buyers and the sellers, as well as the size of their orders. That confidentiality is very attractive to the users of the crossing system. With spreads having narrowed, and given the inability of institutions to display orders in the open marketplace, we have seen our order sizes grow significantly at POSIT vis-à-vis order sizes at the exchanges. I think we will see some modification, and perhaps some formal linkages, between the continuous auction market trading systems and the crossing systems that we run over a period of time, with some addition of price discovery functionality added in the form of discretion to buy or sell at prices away from the mid-point.

DOMOWITZ: Jim Ross of Instinet has been in the crossing business for about eleven years. He has talked to me about bringing crossing to the next level. Jim, will you tell us what you mean by this?

JAMES ROSS: We have built an entire economy and business culture around the continuous trading environment. Continuous trading is the basis for our entire equity market place and while we have grown accustomed to the emotionally satisfying benefits of fast and furious trading, and the almost cannibalistic desire to make money at other people's expense, we have also begun to recognize that these benefits of this roller coaster process may be outweighed by the drawbacks (like market manipulation, front running, excessive price volatility, "pennying" implementation shortfall etc.)

Call market trading addresses, in a large part, many of the inefficiencies and drawbacks of the continuous market. Introducing call market trading, on the other hand, into the bedrock of the well-established continuous environment is a difficult task at best. Business models are developed that are based on continuous trading methodologies and, as a result, are not necessarily suitable for the call market environment, whether it is in enhanced functionality or embracing new technologies. The SROs and Regulators are not necessarily thinking about call markets either. They see call markets as sideshows or exceptions rather than a legitimate piece of the National Market Structure puzzle.

It is quite possible that as these "sideshow" Crossing systems become bigger, they could possibly undermine the primary market upon which they rely for their benchmark pricing. Granted, Instinet Global Crossing is handling only eight to ten million shares in single counted trades but, as we grow, I am becoming worried. If we become too big, if we start handling fifty to one hundred million shares daily, at what point am I drawing price discovery liquidity away from the market? It may already be happening in small or medium size stocks. So the goal must be to integrate call market trading into the National Market Structure.

For this reason, I am extremely supportive of the price discovery auction idea. With the evolution of ATSs, we are at a stage where we could, using price discovery, bring call auctions more into the limelight. The NASDAQ open, IPOs, pending news/halted trading issues or after hours trading, all beg for the benefits of a price discovery call auction.

DOMOWITZ: Bill, you have been trying to move into the auction business in a very sophisticated way with regard to order design. How does your system fit in?

WILLIAM LUPIEN: The biggest disappointment is probably the slow pace with which our customers have been able to understand and to adopt a system that many have said is too sophisticated or too complex to use. There are people in the audience who have said to me privately that they do not know why others find it difficult, because they certainly know how to use it. I will say this. I have been involved with call markets since 1965. The first seventeen years as a specialist. People said earlier today that the openings on the New York Stock Exchange, and on most exchanges in the country, are technically conducted as call markets. We have tried to give the customer, in a sophisticated way, the ability to put in orders that would have two characteristics. One would seek out true price discovery and, as Jim Ross said earlier, the crossing networks really derive their prices from the primary markets. They are looking for a mid-point cross. Our system is designed to allow customers to seek price discovery, which I think is really important if you are going to have sizable trades in the market.

I was a little surprised to hear Bob Schwartz say that maybe only once an hour would be the adequate frequency for a call market. I differ a little bit on that. If two or more parties want to trade in size, the trade should be allowed to happen at any time. I understand that having pre-determined points in time can, in fact, coalesce more orders, but I do not know that artificially setting the time frame is a positive thing.

By the way, we do not know that we have the right solution, either. We have just gone to a fifteen-minute time cycle from a two-minute time cycle, trying to test where that time frame should be. From the Intermarket Trading System's (ITS) standpoint, it has been extraordinarily difficult, but we have integrated a call market with the continuous market. We sweep into each call all of the available liquidity that is represented in the continuous market. When you have a call, everybody participates.

The SEC has essentially given us the go-ahead but, regretfully, the Commission has failed to take on the more difficult issue of the ITS. So, we have ended up with a compromise. Quite frankly, compromises often are not good for anybody. What we had envisioned has been only partially successful.

Dick Grasso[47] at the New York Stock Exchange said he thought it was time to get rid of ITS. I was interested in that, because the NYSE was the only exchange to veto our moving forward on this. We ended up negotiating with the NYSE, and now he wants to get rid of it.

I am in favor of markets, and I do not care if they are continuous markets, periodic call markets, or whatever. Someone said earlier that one size does not fit all. I believe that this is the case. There are times when I probably could have used a 400-share call execution at Knight/TriMark at the mid-point. There have been other times when I would have had to break up my order a hell of a lot to get 400 shares executed each time I wanted to trade.

Perhaps the most frustrating thing is that technology is ahead of what the practices are. Many of you here today know how to use technology far better than we are effectively using it. My wish is that we unfetter the competitive environment so that people can and will use the new technology and improve the markets. That way, everybody will win. We will see multi-billion share markets, which probably is not such a sterling number today.

People want to trade in a variety of ways, maybe even 24-hours a day and seven days a week. Technology is the only way we will be able to do that. I am used to be a specialist, and we had to do this manually many years ago. There is no way we could do it today if we did not have the electronic ability that currently exists. We would not be anywhere near the market volume we are at today. I would encourage more experimentation, more pushing forward. I know most of the markets are trying to do that.

DOMOWITZ: Bruce, can you follow-up? You are the IT guy.

BRUCE WEBER: I will reiterate what Bill was just saying. We tend to be capable of doing something long before it becomes the accepted practice. Securities trading is no different than a lot of other industries, such as book sales or digital content sales, that are possible now on the Internet. People still like to go to malls, however. And people are still paying higher and higher prices for office space in Manhattan.

As an IT person, and as somebody who has been involved in software development and software design, including the development of a trading simulation, this is what I think. With technology or software development, you are faced with trade-offs. The trade-offs often come down to "ease of use" versus "power." A lot of the trading technologies that are not adapted early generally have a lot of power built into them. Ease of use, on the other hand, is generally not a major consideration with respect to initial system design. Some statistics on the Microsoft Office Suite of products illustrate my point. The typical user does not use roughly nineteen out of twenty

[3] Dick Grasso is Chairman and Chief Executive Officer of the New York Stock Exchange.

functions in Microsoft Office. We are only using two to three percent of what is possible. There is a lesson in this. The technology for trading must look at what is happening on the trading desk, which is where the order originates. It must take into account how the order is represented in its most primitive state.

I recently saw some statistics on the Fidelity Magellan Fund. Fidelity has over $100 billion under management. All told, 30 percent of the fund is in the top ten stocks that the fund holds. They have positions in individual stocks of up to three billion, or five billion, and, at times, even more. So, when Bob Stansky, who is running the Magellan Fund, decides he wants to lighten up on Home Depot (or alternatively decides to add to his position in Home Depot), how does he get $3 billion worth of the stock sold or bought? Indeed, trading in this size has got to be very tricky.

The technology that is ultimately going to give us a new call auction, or call auction features, must recognize this challenging situation. The fund manager must make some very high-stakes decisions. What are the ways the traders can support portfolio managers more efficiently, reduce the costs of altering positions, and contribute to better performance? How should that order for $3 billion worth of stock be captured electronically? How should it be directed to where it might best find liquidity and counter parties?

The most interesting developments that could be supportive of call auctions are communication standards and protocols like FIX.[48] FIX was initially set up as just a simple, bilateral communication protocol between Fidelity and Solomon Brothers. It is a standard that could support call auction functions. It could be integrated with the market designs that Ray Killian, Jim Ross, and Bill Lupien operate. Maybe it will become the lingua franca of financial trading.

In that event, market design and market structure become less important than the market's ability to capture some type of a fixed message, and to convert that message into a transaction if the matching orders (liquidity) are there. With shortening settlement cycles, there will be more pressure to develop and adopt these kinds of communication protocols. I am an information systems professor, not an economist or financial markets person. From my perspective, I think the push toward T+1[49] settlement is going to catalyze trading communications protocols, which will in turn improve order management practices and trading, within the next year or two. The

[48] FIX stands for "Financial Information Exchange."

[49] The Securities and Exchange Commission (SEC) has recommended that US financial markets reduce the settlement window from three days after trade date (T+3) to next day or trade date + 1 (T+1). The project's completion date was set at June 2004, but it was pushed up a year to June 2005.

marketplaces and the market designers who figure out how to be the catcher's glove and the preferred liquidity destinations for those FIX messages, and who try to integrate them into their structure, will win the day.

The open, flexible structures will be the most convenient for the users and best for the fund manager. They would give users the chance to see and to find liquidity that might not be on a traditional exchange. At that stage, for example, a trader might use a crossing system, or an ECN, and then preference any remaining part of the order to a market maker.

Call market features will become more practical and better integrated into markets when it is possible for the communication protocols to accommodate the call market design. I am looking for the emergence of call auction principles in systems that will be built around standardized trade communication protocols. This will be a beneficial merger of the plumbing of the trading desks with the mechanics of market facilitation and price discovery at the exchanges, market systems, and broker-dealers.

The merger should combine the execution techniques and capabilities of the OptiMarks, the POSITs, the Instinet Crossing Networks, and the State Street Bond Connects. As the push toward T+1 gets underway and the FIX protocol takes over, the ability to get messages, and orders, and trading interests into a call auction will only grow and drive this innovation in market design.

DOMOWITZ: As a finance guy who has worked in equities derivatives and fixed income to some extent, I believe the design of an automated market does depend on the instruments being traded. This is particularly true for fixed income, an area where people at first tried to take equity systems and turn them into bond systems. A lot of people note that fixed income is very different and, therefore, that the systems used for trading in fixed income must be different than the systems for trading equities.

Andy Howieson has been working on this. My count of fixed income systems, either on the drawing boards or in place, is up to thirty-nine. Andy now claims there are forty-six, which does not include Europe, where some of the bigger developments are occurring.[50] Andy, what kind of design features are important, particularly for fixed income? In other words, what differentiates these things?

ANDREW HOWIESON: The fixed income market is very different from the equity market. That is what State Street's experience has been to

[50] The number of fixed income systems in the US peaked at over 80 around the time of the conference two years ago, according to Howieson. That number has dropped dramatically to less than ten today. One estimate put the number of systems in Europe at about nine.

date. A lot of people on the buyside tell you that there are real problems in the US fixed income markets. Transacting trades in them is far too expensive. As a result, an awful lot of potential transactions actually do not occur. There is marginal, if any, liquidity in many of the instruments. Once you step away from the treasuries and some of the agencies, which are the real center stream of the market, there is precious little liquidity to be found. There are very few mechanisms that help to generate or to maximize whatever liquidity there is. Anonymity is lost the moment you pick up the telephone and talk to a dealer. That is it. The word is out.

There is no real price discovery, unless you have an army of people and make a barrage of telephone calls. You have to call two hundred markets and names to claim that you have achieved any real price discovery.

Our approach has been to let our client base see what we have been doing. We have not gone out of our way to promote a call auction directly. However, once you get into a more detailed explanation, it is clear that a call auction can remedy a great many of the problems in the fixed income market.

Charges, or fees, look a lot different because the cost structure is different than the equities markets. Clearly, there is a temporal aggregation of liquidity in our Bond Connect system, and that absolutely helps. Anonymity exists in our applications, and we offer very deep price discovery. It really is the call mechanism that is making much of this possible (especially price discovery). It is the call mechanism that is helping us to introduce a sophisticated trading methodology that we very much believe helps to maximize liquidity.

But it does not work to sit in front of a busy institutional investor and say, "This call auction thing is great, you should try it." They all think that the continuous market must be better than the call, almost by definition. However, when people see what can be achieved with the call mechanism, they become receptive to the auction process. I know at least half a dozen major institutions whose initial reactions were, "Hmm, we really like what you have been doing with this call thing, but continuous trading has got to be better." Then, after they have really understood what our application can deliver, largely thanks to the call mechanism, their reaction becomes, "Hmm, this call thing really does make sense, at least in the markets that we are talking about."

DOMOWITZ: Susan Woodward has been down in the trenches trying to make calls an integral part of the capital-raising business at the primary level. What has your experience been at OffRoad Inc.?

SUSAN WOODWARD: At OffRoad,[51] we have focused on the private part of the capital market. Why? Because that is where it is possible to innovate and not run into SEC rules. W.R. Hambrecht (I admire him enormously for his bravery in trying to bring efficient market pricing to IPOs) has this same problem with SEC rules. The Commission will not allow him to run an auction with any kind of feedback to bidders or others during the auction process. Because he is selling registered securities, he cannot show the investors what fraction of the deal has been sold. He cannot show the investors what the price is, or let them know when price changes, and he certainly could not show the investors every single order.

Because we at OffRoad are dealing in private securities and do not have to abide by those SEC rules, at OffRoad we are able to provide feedback on both fill (the fraction of a deal that is sold) and price (which only moves up with additional orders once an entire deal is sold). While we provide feedback on fill and price, we do not show every order. Providing information on price and fill goes a long way towards informing the market.

I have another point to make. Everybody who has spoken today has been so nice. The most cynical statements have come from people suggesting that the opposition to change is a competitive, strategic move, rather than a real concern about market design. Will no one suggest that it really is SEC rules that are inhibiting innovation?

The SEC's rules inhibit many things – not only running an auction for individual investors and providing feedback about prices during the price discovery process. They also inhibit simple things like putting an offering document on the Internet with hypertext links. Putting an offering document on the Internet with hypertext links is an illegal practice for an initial public offering, because the offering has to be reviewed by the SEC and the SEC does not have the time to review the hypertext. In an OffRoad offering, the offering document is up there on the Web site. It is formatted in a beautiful template that makes it easy to understand. It is full of links, because people do not sit down and read an offering document page after page. They get to a point and say, "Oh, there are some numbers here on this page." Then they want to click and move and perhaps see the numbers in greater detail, then, later, go back and read some more. People's reading habits have become impatient. They do not keep reading to the end. They skip around, and the Internet takes advantage of the process in an important way.

But if you want to do a public offering that acknowledges and harnesses these behaviors, the SEC would stand in your way. At OffRoad, we hope to demonstrate that it is better to have an auction with a feedback, and that it is

[51] At the time of the conference, Susan Woodward was on the senior management team at OffRoad Capital.

better to have a beautiful and very usable template. Both promote market efficiency. Instead of standing in the way, the SEC should promote feedback and usability.

DOMOWITZ: So, Bill Lupien, what do you think of the SEC?

LUPIEN: What do I think of the Commission? It is my regulator (laughter). Actually, I wish the SEC would use many of the excess funds that they return to the Treasury to bring in more people so that it could respond to what Susan just said. The talent at the agency is good, but they have a tremendous workload. For the life of me, I cannot understand why the Commission sees it fit to return funds to the treasury when, in fact, everyone in the industry is complaining about the slowness of improving the regulation. It is not just with regard to call markets. It is in market structure more generally. It is in every area, and we are all hampered as a result.

DOMOWITZ: Attempts to regulate market structure obviously impact the business. I would like to get into that a little more.

WEBER: Yes, clearly. Exchanges, ECNs, and entrepreneurial developers of new market systems develop market structures and trading rules to compete for order flow. They are also aware that the SEC approvals, no-action letters, etc., determine whether they have a chance to compete, and whether there will be limitations in terms of the time of operation, volumes, disclosure, etc. on the operation of their systems.

You asked about how structures are changing. One thing will dramatically impact the way call auctions operate. It is the improvement of the mathematics of optimization. When you can submit large lists of securities to the auction for crossing, you do not want to be cherry-picked on the cross. From a POSIT users' perspective, you do not want to have only the easy executions take place, or have momentum issues to deal with, such as a sharp price movement near the crossing. To help with this, users can take order flow to the crossing and submit a list of constraints, along with the order list, that allow a user to maintain a buy-sell balance, limit tracking error, and so on. That is going to improve the environment as well, and that is an area where a lot of work is being done now.

One other point that I would like to make relates to the discussion about why call markets would not be attractive to retail buyers. Retail buyers are basically instant gratification seekers. They want to buy right now and sell right now, and they are not going to wait for any hourly crosses. Some of the larger institutional customers need to be more discriminating because of how they conduct their business, or because of the size of their orders. Jim Ross referred to the critical point at which a call auction becomes a price discovery activity. Academics have been talking about that for a few years. As total volume expands in the continuous market, that topic moves a bit further out on the horizon.

DOMOWITZ: Bill, this notion of increased sophistication, what kind of weight should be given to it? You have made a lot of investment in that area.

LUPIEN: Ease of use is a major issue. If people cannot use something, it does not make a difference how good it is. If they are unable to use it, they do not get the benefit. I have underestimated in the past how people would respond to something. We all look at the world from our own vantage point, and we often assume that others do the same.

I remember meeting with someone who was very sophisticated and extraordinarily wealthy. We were sitting down to explain how OptiMark would work, and this person said, "I don't really use a computer." My partner said, "I can show you how to do that. You take the mouse, you move the cursor up to this spot, and you click." This sophisticated person picked the mouse up, held it against the screen, and clicked. Honest to God, that is the truth. Right away I said to myself, "This is not going to work" (laughter). "This person is not going to get there."

It is a real eye-opener when you come across this. If you are going to move ahead, you must break out of the conventional environment. But I have heard people say, "You know what your problem is? You are always too far out in front." Maybe that is true. It is frustrating. When you are out in front, you cannot figure out why others are not following you.

But to get somewhere (academics certainly understand this), you must think out of the box. You have to cajole, push, and pull, whatever you can, to get the masses to go along with you. OptiMark has done a very good job of educating a lot of people as to how call markets work, and about how technology can change the business. Sometimes we have seen users' eyes glaze over. The mathematical side is something that most of us probably would not want to have to deal with.[52] But, in fact, if you want optimal outcomes, the tools are there. Many of the people in this audience know. The question is, can you get the masses there?

We attempted to integrate a call market with the continuous market. We did so by taking the retail and institutional orders that are resident in the continuous market. We would sweep them into a call market in an

[52] OptiMark, having failed to generate sufficient liquidity, did not succeed as a facility of the Nasdaq Stock Market. In an early 2002 interview one panelist, Ian Domowitz, currently a managing director at ITG, contended that the consensus view was that OptiMark was too complicated for traders to use. In most cases, traders first took several hours of class instruction on OptiMark. Dealer's reluctance to adopt OptiMark should not be attributed to OptiMark's competitive threat to intermediaries, Domowitz said. If that was the case, then ECNs would not have succeeded in handling up to 50 percent of Nasdaq trade volume, he contended.

aggregated form that allows, let us say, non-sophisticated people's orders (retail and so forth) to be included, just as they are on the New York Stock Exchange floor every single morning. No one questions the value of having a call market, at the opening, on the New York Stock Exchange, or on the American Stock Exchange, or on any other exchange today. Retail orders as small as 100 shares and institutional orders of up to a million shares or more, all get integrated into it together.

DOMOWITZ: Jim, you are working with a variety of what I would call "exchange services."[53] Where does a call fit into the business plan of that type of organization?

ROSS: We have been trying to provide a service while educating people on crossing. There are ten of us. Five of us are sales people. We talk to people, press them, push them. We call them at night to see if they are coming into our cross, in case they forgot, and that is usually what they end up doing. But pretty much, we have not really sat down and said, "What is it that you want to do?"

In 1991, the New York Stock Exchange introduced its after-hours crossing sessions, which they still run. I was scared. I said to myself, "There goes my job." I was also thinking that this might legitimize us a bit, that it might give us some visibility. Perhaps we may gain some credibility with people, because an exchange was now running a crossing system. Maybe somebody from the New York Stock Exchange can attest to this, but the Exchange's facility has basically turned into a basket-trading system. It is not really a matching system. One of the complaints that I have heard is that you have to go through a member service. It is the same old structure, the same old thing. What has ended up happening is that some people basically get their orders shopped.

Just like OptiMark, we looked at the crossing and call auctions in our business strategy. We must figure out how to avoid writing our business strategy based on the old premise and the old paradigms of the continuous system. That is why I have again asked our SROs and our regulators to be open to the concept of call market capabilities as they work to reform and evolve their market regulations and rules. They have actually been very generous with us over the years. That is primarily because they have been focusing on the real-time trading system at Instinet.

I worry that there would be additional regulation. Steve Wunsch at the Arizona Stock Exchange has a limited volume exemption. We have exemptions all around. At some point, we need to get into the mainstream (and out of the exemption stream). We need to be part of the broader

[53] The term, "exchange services," refers to the various facilities offered by an exchange, such as quote services, execution capabilities, hosting functions.

structure of the markets. If we can get there, we are going to have to accept that we will be regulated. But we have to work with the regulators to make sure that it is a sensible, competitive environment.

DOMOWITZ: Do call markets give some kind of a competitive edge in this business?

WOODWARD: For us, it is essential. This is because we are making two kinds of pitches. For individual investors, we are offering access, period. We are offering a kind of access that they did not have before. For small institutions, we are providing a kind of access to private equity that they did not have.

When we first began the marketing program, people were extremely nervous about our pricing. These people were foot draggers. Now, they have come around completely and see that the price discovery process helps and does not hurt them.

Here is the second pitch. To attract issuers to the OffRoad market, market pricing is a key feature. The issuers sit down with a term sheet from OffRoad, plus a couple from venture capitalists, and maybe one from an investment bank. The term sheets from the venture capitalists and the other investment banks are all fixed price. With OffRoad, the term sheet specifies the price where the offering begins. Price can only go up from there. The issuer might be able to sell a stock at a higher price than its initial offering price on the OffRoad term sheet. To do this, the call market is essential.

We are building a secondary market that we plan to unroll after the 144 required year has expired for our first issuers.[54] It will be the only organized market where you can trade private equity in the secondary market, in a quarterly or semi-annual, single-priced auction.[55] The intellectual property was sold to the NYPPe[56] which so far as I know has not used it to run an auction as of April 2002.

[54] Rule 144 specifies that if you buy an unregistered security and hold it for a year before attempting to sell it, there is no presumption that you bought the security in order to resell it. If you had bought it to resell it, it should have been registered.

[55] Alas, what happened is that although OffRoad closed on $50 million in April 2000, the marketing people had spent it all by April 2001. OffRoad could raise no more money and ceased operations in August 2001.

[56] The NYPPe (New York Private Placement Exchange) operates a global electronic communication network (ECN) for trading and issuance of restricted securities and interests in private funds. The Company provides specialized execution, information, research, and communication services for private, 144, 144a, and public transactions for institutional and accredited individual investors, issuers, broker-dealers, and market makers.

An interesting side note, it is now clear that the market did very well in pricing issues. The issues the market put the highest prices on were indeed the best, and the ones it did with reluctance were the weakest. Whatever the bankers and other experts knew, the investors brought something additional to the marketplace.

DOMOWITZ: Andy, why are you going with a call? Are you going to compete with dealers on the basis of a call market?

HOWIESON: I do not represent the whole of State Street. We have other endeavors as well. The part of State Street that I do represent, the information partnerships (which is about to be called Advanced Auctions, LLC), is absolutely focused on developing and deploying combined value call auctions to create new securities trading markets around the world.[57] We are doing this because we think it is a very exciting technology, a very exciting methodology.

We fundamentally believe that major improvements are needed in securities markets around the world. We are very receptive to the sellside, but our core call client base is the buyside.

If you look from the top down at securities markets around the world, fragmentation is incredible for the year 2000. Think of what an investor manager's process looks like. It is very tight, very integrated. It is often a very sophisticated process that uses a number of advanced tools. However, portfolio-level trading decisions must be disseminated into all these unconnected securities markets, and in most cases there is no ability to link those orders in any way.

Technology can help us to bring these markets together in an organized and effective manner that will improve the state of execution globally. That is very much at the core of our game plan.

DOMOWITZ: The core of the game plan, as was pointed out in the last session, is in part the ability to handle order flow. In the few minutes left in this session, let us move back to the design issue. I will now reveal my bias with respect to continuous markets. It is not clear to me exactly how the demand for immediacy, broadly defined, is being served. I do not mean to imply that I want to execute my order within the next minute.

There are a variety of designs for call markets. If people were actually drawing pictures, we would see many varieties in terms of algorithms,

[57] Combined value refers to a methodology used in the Bond Connect system. It was a means by which multiple securities could be traded simultaneously together in a way that the pricing affects each security. For example, an investor could buy something and could sell something else as one transaction. The various possibilities could have an affect on the outcome. Bond Connect is believed to have had the first application of that methodology in any financial marketplace. The term "combined value" does not cover basket trading.

transparency, and the way information can be displayed. But something that certainly has spurred electronic continuous markets on, more overseas than here, is that the role of the market maker has never really disappeared.

We could certainly dis-intermediate the brokers whose function it is to provide access to the market, but in most thriving electronic markets that I know of in the continuous world, we still have market makers. They make markets on the computer.

They may have special screens that allow them to post two-sided markets – bids and asks. The electronic market itself has not done away with that. Market makers supply liquidity. They commit capital. I would like to ask the panel whether or not you see a role for the market maker in an electronic call auction. How can this role be integrated within a call auction environment? What do you do with the residuals – what is left over and unexecuted – after the call?

WEBER: If you look at how people have traditionally talked about technology and markets, it is almost always tied in with the issue of dis-intermediation. Some people are middlemen and IT may cut them out. That is, to some extent, always the job of the technology person. But the thinking is simplistic.

To get their executions done, institutions need somebody on the other side committing capital. That is what a lot of the work in market microstructure shows, and what institutions themselves say. You are not always going to match up one natural buyer with one natural seller. Things do not work out that way in practice. Given the needs of investors, intermediation will be needed, but it will be in different forms and to different extents than in the past. It has been said that, "banking is necessary; banks are not." The concept applies to market makers.

So, we are moving toward a much more openly connected world of markets. Information and market functionality is going to move up the food chain all the way back to the buyside fund manager's trading desks. The market structures and the call auction designs will have to look less like closed, stand-alone systems, and more like software APIs.[58] The hurdles that are being overcome are the incompatible messaging standards between brokers and customers, and between brokers and markets. Markets, brokers, and customers will eventually have end-to-end software based on trading system APIs. This will enable order messages to go out, and to be converted into other formats when necessary. For instance, a FIX message can become

[58] API stands for "Application Programming Interface."

a CMS[59] message on the NYSE, although CMS initially was not capable of handling FIX messages.

The job for the market designers of the future will be figuring out how to get Bob Stansky's trader to take whatever representation he has of the Magellan portfolio interests that day, and be the catcher's mitt for it. Some of the developments with FIX, as well as XML,[60] could enable you to specify a number of different ways you want your order to be handled. Most of the evidence suggests traders want to find liquidity for their orders, and are not overly concerned with the type of counter party.

For instance, ITG's POSIT had an "institution-only box" that could be checked off to restrict an institutional client's order to match only with another institution's order, and not with orders from a broker/dealer. I understand that not many of ITG's customers checked it off.

DOMOWITZ: The point is that market makers are not necessarily dis-intermediated by electronic markets. In electronic continuous auctions, you do have market makers, so it is a misconception to think of market makers solely as Nasdaq dealers. That is not true of all asset classes, and it is not even true across all equities. Market makers commit capital to the market and they earn something for that. They supply immediacy where there is a demand, and they charge for it. I don't see why that should go away, regardless of the market structure, unless someone can figure out how to design an electronic market that also manages to take one side of a trade when no one else wants to do so.

I don't believe that electronic markets in and of themselves can dis-intermediate the market maker function. The story is different for much more liquid issues, however. If I want to trade Microsoft, I probably don't need a market maker. I can get that done in the open market very easily – and I can get it done on electronic systems. But if I want to trade something where the average daily volume is very low, and I want to trade, say, 50 percent of the average daily volume, I may not be able to do so without someone who is willing to commit capital to the trade. So it is not the market structure itself that dis-intermediates the capital commitment (although the market structure may make it more or less difficult to make money committing capital). This, however, does not dis-intermediate that function. One reason I bring this up is that it is a huge misconception that somehow electronic markets are substitutes for the commitment of capital.

[59] CMS stands for "Common Message Switch." It is a store-and-forward message-switching device that connects member firms to exchange systems.

[60] XML stands for "Extensible Markup Language." It is the universal format for structured documents and data on the Web.

WEBER: My guess is that the role of intermediaries, especially on the market making capital commitment side, will remain strong. Their role will remain strong even in a marketplace where we have lots of linked markets, both continuous and call. Those market-making firms that survive will be the ones that figure out how to handle the volumes and to manage the risks of having inventories in these stocks. They will do more than simply set up market designs and hope to find the natural other side, both buyer and seller. They will figure out ways to provide incentives for investors to come in and pick up residuals, and to take some risks by buying or selling inventory. They will do so, not as long-term investors, but as if they were dealers.

I want to stress that mechanisms must be in place to provide incentives for a market maker to pick up the slack, when the natural buyers and the natural sellers are not there at the same points in time.

DOMOWITZ: How do you manage that?

KILLIAN: If anybody in this room, or anybody on this panel, was given $400 million tomorrow, and we told them to build a market making system, we would not see the specialist system reinvented as it currently exists. It would probably be a computer-driven system. It would be a system that handles volume well, that wraps risk management technology around specialist or system price discovery and, most likely, it would be funded by a third party for the absorption of risk and the supply of liquidity. But it would also be connected to all of the other various venues that you must reach in order to attract critical mass. That is the best edge of all. The sophistication of the technology today leads me to think that this is probably the way some of the major firms will end up running their market making operations over the next couple of years.

DOMOWITZ: So, Andy, can you make markets at Bond Connect?

HOWIESON: Absolutely we can. We have had several broker/dealers who have told us that they intend to make markets by actively quoting in the system. However, let us be very careful about what we mean by market makers and market making. A number of broker/dealers have told us that they will make markets, that they will put in buy and sell orders, in both directions on a number of securities.

This makes enormous sense for the dealer community. They probably see this sort of endeavor as a good use of their capital. What does not make sense, for example, in the fixed income context, is moving a security effectively between two buyside institutions, something we often loosely refer to as being a market maker. Assume Fidelity wants to buy a security, and that Putnam wants to sell the same security. In the classic fixed-income market, this action involves at least two broker deals and two inter-dealer brokers. There is an awful lot of friction and an awful lot of cost involved in doing a very simple transaction. This is one of the reasons why the fixed income markets are not working well.

The dealers are not pleased about having to commit capital in that way. They would rather commit the capital to do something that requires a little more knowledge and a little more risk undertaking. Frankly, some of their activities are better served by good automated applications. However, is it still possible for a dealer to make markets intelligently in that sort of application? Absolutely.

DOMOWITZ: Some questions from the floor?

HAROLD BRADLEY, American Century Investment Management [From the Floor]: I am troubled that this is probably my fourth Bob Schwartz call market conference where, as a buyside trader and portfolio manager, it makes an eminent amount of sense to me. I look at the studies we have seen over the last four or five years, such as Economides and Schwartz's paper on immediacy, that have asked about what the buyside would really tolerate.[61] What is the buyside demanding from the market?

What they want is price-time priority, anonymity, and control over their orders. What we see is persistence by the buyside to do the same old things. We talk about the renting of capital. It costs money to rent a broker's capital to trade. Frankly, I do not need a broker's capital on an ECN to do a very large block of stock. We have got a lot of data to support that contention. But people still want to do the old thing, which is to rent the capital, let the broker turn around and work it off in the market using an ECN, and charge a high price to do it.

When will the buyside understand that it is in their best interests to use a call market? Secondly, isn't it a fact that the sellside will never use a call market because that ultimately takes them right out of the middle?

HOWIESON: In response to your second question, no, I do not think so. If it could be done – and there are probably 50 sellside people in this room who are going to shoot me for this – if it could be done without impacting other business and without it looking like a retreat, I think a lot of sellside players would be very happy to no longer be involved in moving a security from Fidelity to Putnam Fixed Income Security. I think that they would actually participate in the right sort of electronic call market. Certainly, the evidence that we have so far seen suggests that this would be the case.

[61] "Equity Trading Practices and Market Structure: Assessing Asset Managers' Demand for Immediacy, with Nicholas Economides, *Financial Markets, Institutions and Instruments,* Vol. 4, No. 4, 1995, pp. 1 - 46. Also published under the title, "Making the Trade: Equity Trading Practices and Market Structure," Report of the TraderForum Research Service of the Institutional Investor, Spring 1994.

How receptive is the buyside going to be? I think that it takes a bit of time. We have found that it takes time. It takes time to let people see and understand how the market works.

HAROLD BRADLEY [From the Floor]: Does it take regulation?

HOWIESON: From the fixed income perspective, at this point, I cannot say that it would require special regulation.

KILLIAN: If you will grant that POSIT is a call auction of some kind, about 115 broker/dealers who participate have research orders and are searching for liquidity. I would say that brokers are willing to use a call if it serves their purpose as well as the clients' purpose. The buyside is becoming a lot more sophisticated about how to take the risk premium out of bids and offers that brokers are using with the technology that is available today. I see more major institutional desks handling the risk very carefully. They are handling it very intelligently.

DOMOWITZ: That is a good note to end on. I would like to thank the panel for a very informative session.

CHAPTER 5: DARWINISM VS. PROTECTIONISM IN THE US EQUITY MARKETS; THE CASE FOR REAL COMPETITION[62]

Douglas Atkin
Efficient Frontiers[63]

One of the great mysteries in life is why things change and do not remain the same. Since a lot of physics and biology is based on various ideas of "balance," it turns out that this question is not as silly as it seems. Since it's hard to manage things you do not understand, the insights from nature's change process should help us chart evolutions in the man made world, evolutions that include the equity markets. It turns out, in fact, that nature has a lot it can teach us.

As everybody knows, in the natural world, a primary driving force is Darwin's "natural selection". This is the process in which genes associated with superior performance multiply in the gene pool at the expense of the weaker genes whose presence leads to less successful outcomes.

The power of natural selection is incremental, operating over thousands of generations. Small improvements accumulate over time in the same way that compound interest can turn a penny into a fortune.

In the food chain we know that "slow prey get eaten." Often, survival is as dependent on being able to overtake your own kind as it is on overwhelming your enemies.

Another important consequence of natural selection is "co-evolution." That is the tendency of species to evolve in tandem. In co-evolution theory

[62] This chapter is based on the transcript of the conference, The Electronic Call Auction: New Answers to Old Questions, held at Baruch College/CUNY on May 16, 2000.

[63] At the time of the conference, Douglas Atkin was President and CEO of Instinet Corporation.

the frog and the fly he eats are bound together inextricably. If the frog develops better eyesight and a faster tongue, then the fly will be pushed to develop superior evasive tactics. This leads to a sort of "arms race" in which all parties advance, but the balance of power often remains unchanged. This interplay of interdependence and adversity characterizes the business world.

The second part of the evolution story -- which sets the stage for the interactions I just described -- is environmental change. Habitats are always changing, but they usually do so very, very slowly. However, once in a while the pace picks up dramatically. That is when things get very interesting because that is when fundamental change occurs.

The biological record clearly shows that shifts in environment are just as important as competitive natural selection in shaping the process of change.

1. HOW BUSINESSES CHANGE

While the process of change in business is different -- firms lack genes, for instance, and change often occurs over a more accelerated time scale than the millions of years required for biological evolution -- the underlying processes in both have many similarities. Environmental change sets the context as the interplay of competition and cooperation animates the action.

I'm sure that I don't have to explain how it works. In the natural world, slow prey is eaten. In business, it is called Mergers and Acquisitions but, fortunately, nobody has to die. Even when people are forced to jump ship, they are likely to be saved by a golden parachute, if you'll pardon the mixed metaphor.

On the environmental side, the major driving forces are technology and regulation. The former changes the rules of engagement, while the latter establishes the parameters of engagement.

2. WHAT ARE DIGITAL MARKETS?

Let me turn to the specifics of the markets. Since ancient times, buyers and sellers have met in a common place to conduct business. As we all know, such meeting-places are not just about logistical efficiency, although they clearly serve that purpose. They are also about the all-important processes of price discovery and resource allocation.

Historically, as market participants have increased in number, direct contact between buyers and sellers became impossible. The role of the market had to change from being a meeting-place of principals to a meeting-place of intermediaries. Since the interests of middlemen are not identical to those of the investor -- in fact their interests may be in competition -- various forms of disciplinary measures have always been required to ensure fairness and to prevent abuse. In a nutshell, this pretty much describes where we are today.

An e-market, in contrast, returns us to many of the economic benefits of the traditional markets without the typical costs and risks of intermediation. An e-market provides a direct connection between buyers and sellers while imposing a strict regime for the interactions between them. Electronic interconnections are simply far easier to monitor than telephone, human-to-human, or paper-based transactions. And with the Internet and modern computing, the number of participants is virtually unlimited.

It must be said, however, that in providing these benefits the e-markets raise a very important question: whose interests are to be optimized by the evolving market's design? Investors and issuers on one hand or traditional middlemen and market operators on the other? This is a very important question, and it's right at the core of the current market structure debate.

Personally, I think it's been clear for some time that the legacy intermediary roles simply cannot exist in their old forms in an e-commerce world. The purpose of my biological metaphor is to make clear that this is not an issue that is likely to disappear. In fact, evolution has always led to both extinction events and to tremendous innovation. Nature reminds us that just because a species is dominant in one set of circumstances, it doesn't give it legacy rights in another. On the other hand, we should not expect anyone to quietly pass from the stage without a fight.

I'm not saying, of course, that traditional institutions should disappear. I'm saying that their survival should be determined by their capacity to adapt and compete, and not by their ability to use rules and regulations to preserve legacy advantages. Any form of protectionism always comes out of somebody's pocket. In this case, it's the pockets of investors. What is important to realize is that all investors will soon have the ability to place their money in any market around the world. For the first time, people will have a real choice.

Let me talk about what I think such a new world requires and some of the problems that hinder the competitiveness of US markets on a global scale.

3. REQUIREMENTS FOR EFFICIENT MARKETS

I believe 5 critical requirements are necessary to allow efficient electronic markets to compete with the best in the world.

First, a market should treat all participants without discrimination in a fair and equitable manner. A key aspect of fairness is the degree to which all orders are treated the same by the market. There should be no reason for any party to step ahead of someone else's previously entered best price order by filling others at the same price while ignoring the price-setter. Both of our main markets permit these practices which clearly favor certain intermediaries and hurt investors.

The second requirement is the protection of the information value of the customer's order itself. One of the biggest economic burdens borne by large institutions is the market impact costs associated with inadvertently revealing their trading intentions to intermediaries. An analogous problem arises when retail customers innocently give intermediaries an information advantage through the accumulation of their overnight orders. In both cases, certain intermediaries trade against their own customers. Most clients are paying more than they should because of the lack of standing of client limit orders. While these practices are most of the time well within the rules, rules that allow this are bad for investors precisely to the degree that they are good for the intermediaries.

The third requirement is order book transparency. The economic evidence from various electronic markets suggests that markets tend to work best when their order books are transparent. However, the transparency problem we have in this marketplace is two-fold. First, and most obvious, is that investors should see the depth of the book. Second, more important and much more subtle, is that because investors' orders do not receive the appropriate standing in our marketplace, investors seriously lack the incentive to display their orders in the book. Therefore our books are not as deep as they ought to be.

The reason for this is simple: When an investor "displays" an order on an exchange for public dissemination, the investor is giving away valuable economic information. The investor, however, does not receive the appropriate economic value in return. If an intermediary can have the right of first refusal before the investor gets a trade executed then why should investors wish to display, or for that matter, be forced to display their prices? This is the substantive issue with transparency. What we need is a regime that gives investors an appropriate economic deal for displaying orders. If we do, then our open order books will be deep.

Fourth, the market must be able to respond rapidly to customer orders, and it must do so consistently across customer groups. Clearly, in a volatile market, quickly having one's intentions acted on is a key element of trading performance. Furthermore, if speed of execution is variable across customer groups, it's just another form of bias, since it inevitably leads to poorer executions or to none at all. Failure to execute is just another form of trading cost.

Finally, to the greatest extent possible the markets must operate consistently, with true costs and benefits rather than cross-subsidies and special deals. For instance, the economic performance of both of the main [US] markets -- the NYSE and Nasdaq -- is based upon their exclusive rights to charge fees for market data and regulation. What we need is a market that doesn't tinker on the periphery with complex fee structures. We need a market that levels the playing field by returning to basic economic principles.

This brings me to my recommendations.

4. FIXING NASDAQ

As you can probably tell, I'm a believer in the benefits of competition in achieving the best results. The biological metaphor teaches us that unleashing competition is most important during those times when environmental conditions change. The evolutionary record shows such times to be particularly rich periods of innovation. In business, ironically, this is just the moment that vested interests tend to resort to the highest degrees of protectionism. It is as if legacy institutions like our national markets represent the great American Buffalo that deserve special dispensation. I just don't buy it and neither should you, especially with Nasdaq becoming a privately capitalized, for-profit company.

As a way of bringing my talk to a conclusion, then, I'd like to tell you what I think should happen in the US markets in the trading of Nasdaq stocks - the environment in which some of the world's most successful technology companies such as Amazon, Cisco, Intel, and Yahoo! trade. Ironically, these companies, which symbolize the highest levels of technological prowess and innovation, are traded in a relatively low tech, anti-competitive manner.

Although there are many details I could bore you with, let me stick to the fundamental, bottom-line: what we have vs. what we need in Nasdaq.

First, what we have is really quite interesting. Many pundits seem to feel that Nasdaq has a lot of competition for the trading of its shares. The facts show something completely different: that Nasdaq controls 100% of the market share in the trading of its stocks. Why? That is a good question. ECNs that some see as competitors to Nasdaq are forced to operate under Nasdaq's infrastructure and regulatory authority. There is presently no framework for competing stock exchanges in the Nasdaq world. ECNs have to report all their trades to Nasdaq, display their quotes to Nasdaq, have their fees controlled by Nasdaq, route/receive orders through SelectNet and only give market data to Nasdaq. In essence, ECNs are frustrated exchanges that want to be set free. True competition is being crushed because our regulatory environment does not allow these ECN "competitors" a way to break out from under Nasdaq's monopoly, a way to operate on an equal playing field. It is ironic to me that while there is a lot of legitimate criticism of ITS in the listed arena, at least a framework exists for exchanges competing for NYSE shares. Nasdaq itself IS the ITS of Nasdaq shares.

It is also critical to remember that Nasdaq was never and is not yet a stock exchange. It is, by its own account, a "market of markets" that provides a centralized price bulletin board and order routing facility to its members. Nasdaq's historic role has never been to provide a matching system or exchange to its participants. Now Nasdaq wants to construct – via its SuperMontage proposal – a competing matching service. This represents a major change in Nasdaq's role in the marketplace.

Nasdaq has a monopoly in many areas. It is essential, therefore, to have open and fair competition between competing trading venues *before* Nasdaq becomes a for-profit company which has its own competitive ECN. Over the coming few months, if Nasdaq is permitted to use its SRO status with the government's blessing to radically tilt the playing field by being allowed to build its own ECN, then real competition and investors' interests will be seriously impaired.

Here is an analogy that illustrates the present competitive position of Nasdaq: If the US Postal Service had said to Federal Express at the dawn of overnight delivery: "You can compete with us, but you have to use the post office's delivery system and you have to wait until after we get our own overnight service up and running. Also, by the way, we're using your tax money to build and subsidize our new overnight delivery business. We're going to force you to use our clunky delivery system for your business until we get our new technologies implemented."

If Nasdaq's recently proposed SuperMontage – the foundation of its new business initiative – is really good for the markets, then investors and intermediaries will embrace it in a world of competing stock exchanges. The only way to make the SuperMontage truly voluntary is to give investors a true choice of markets to send their orders to. However, if the markets reject this new idea in favor of something else, then I say welcome Nasdaq to the real world of competition. The key is we need competing markets and the SEC needs to ensure this now.

5. CONCLUSION

In comparison to what we have now, a competing electronic market system is a far simpler and economically superior way of bringing buyers and sellers together. It would be less expensive and it would be fairer.

There is another compelling reason to make this change. The world's electronic markets can, and inevitably will, compete with each other on the global stage as venues for providing investors with the best trading performance and issuers with the lowest cost of capital.

It is easy for us in the US to be lazy about this since we don't have real competition within or between our national exchanges, and foreign-based exchanges can't effectively compete here. However, if recent history teaches us a lesson, it is that these anti-competitive barriers will be eroded by the powers of natural selection and evolution. In just a few months, for example, Frankfurt stole the German bond futures business from London because of the superior efficiency of its electronic platform. As unlikely as it seems, the same thing could happen with our high-tech stocks.

In sum, we are at an important juncture in the evolution of our markets. It is clear to me that we have a basic choice about whether we will let competitive forces get on with market evolution or whether we will try to out-guess mother nature by way of protectionism. By now, you probably know where I stand, and I hope some of you have been encouraged to stand with me as a voice for more broad-sweeping change.

CHAPTER 6: VIEW FROM A DERIVATIVES EXCHANGE[64]

William Brodsky
Chicago Board Options Exchange

For those who are not as steeped in the options business as you may be in the stock market, I'll briefly highlight what's going on in our industry; I'll give you some general thoughts on my view of call markets versus continuous markets; and lastly, I'll focus on one aspect of call markets, and, in particular, how they relate to the options business.

Let me begin by just saying that CBOE was the pioneer of listed options 27 years ago. For those who don't remember how small the options business was when we started, on our first day in April of 1973, our volume was a total of 911 contracts. There was a gentleman on our board from a firm in New York who thought options were a very good idea and that the standardized options business would revolutionize the investment world. Two years ago, on our 25th anniversary, I invited that man, Robert Rubin, the then Secretary of the Treasury, to come visit the Exchange as the keynote speaker for our anniversary luncheon. Bob agreed and in his remarks at the luncheon said that CBOE's creation of a standardized options business was the most important development that could have happened to Goldman Sachs back in the early 70's.

For those of you who may not remember, in those days, firms were just beginning to engage in block trading. The problem was the markets were not very deep, they were not very liquid, and certainly, you could not do a lot of blocks on the floor of the New York Stock Exchange, or anywhere else, for that matter. This lack of liquidity made it difficult for firms like Goldman Sachs to take on a large position to facilitate a customer in a

[64] This chapter is based on the transcript of the conference, The Electronic Call Auction: New Answers to Old Questions, held at Baruch College/CUNY on May 16, 2000.

particular stock. But with the advent of options, the Goldmans, Merrills, Salomons, etc. benefited because they had the opportunity to hedge their positions.

Thus, for the first time in the securities business, the concept of hedging became a reality, and it was a very significant development. Today, the majority of the world's major exchanges trade options.

To provide some additional perspective, when CBOE started in 1973, we traded options on 16 companies -- IBM, General Electric, Coca-Cola, etc. We now trade options on more than 1,500 separate companies. The number of stock options, combined with the multitude of calls, puts, strike prices, and expiration dates gives us in excess of 120,000 different series. This is a staggering number that has developed over the past two-and-a-half decades. CBOE also trades over 40 different indexes. The most important of those are the Nasdaq-100 Index®, the Dow Jones Industrial Average℠, the S&P 500® Index, the S&P 100® Index, and the Russell 2000® Index.

The markets, although still floor-based, are highly electronic at CBOE. Over 90 percent of our customer orders are routed or executed electronically, while 39 percent are now executed with no human intervention. And, electronic market maker terminals handle 95 percent of the trades on the floor. If you visit our trading floor, the lack of shouting and paper strewn about the floor is almost amazing to see, especially for those of you who remember the way floors used to be or envision what a trading floor "should" look like.

The options business now represents 70 percent of all the quotation traffic -- that includes stocks, bonds and options -- in the United States! Again, one of the reasons for this is due to the number of series for each individual security.

To put that in further perspective, if you go to the New York Stock Exchange, they might list 3,000 securities. If you go to the Nasdaq, maybe it's 4,000 securities. But at our options exchange, we're talking about over 120,000 series of separate securities to trade. As a result, our quotation traffic is enormous. During a typical trading day at CBOE, over 25 million quotes are generated. This relates, in large part, to the difference between continuous markets or a call market, because if you have continuous markets, then you're going to be producing substantially more quotes.

A brief word on volume and what's transpired recently. At the four options exchanges in the United States today, almost 61 million contracts with a premium value of approximately $56 billion traded last month. At CBOE, our volume averaged a million and a half contracts a day, a far cry from those 911 contracts back in 1973. Our volume in April is up 32 percent against last year, due primarily to the fact that we have seen significantly increased competition among the exchanges.

I see my colleague and old friend, David Krell, in the audience. Dave is the president and CEO of the International Securities Exchange (ISE), which will become the fifth US options exchange next month. The ISE is going to begin trading options as the first non-floor-based options exchange. ISE's impending launch has spurred a wave of change in our business in terms of fees, competition, multiple listings and upgrading of electronic trading systems.

With this proper perspective on the options industry as background, I'd like to address my personal feelings on the virtues of continuous and call markets. I've been involved, with financial exchanges and markets for a long time. I was taken by the paper written by the good professor that is the nucleus of today's conference -- urging that we have call markets, almost as a replacement for continuous markets. My initial reaction was this: I've grown up in a world where continuous markets seem to have worked well, and with the technology that we have today, seem to be working better than ever.

Many new markets start off as call markets and, as liquidity develops, graduate to the continuous market concept. I think that improved technology, combined with today's complicated strategies, almost mandate continuous markets over call markets. I think of what has happened in the last 15 years or so in terms of indexation, basket trading, and intermarket trading, and I cannot imagine how that would happen in a pure call market environment in the US today. And now, with additional factors, such as order handling rules, market linkages, the growth of ECNs, improved market transparency and the speed with which trading is conducted, the need for a call market, except in unusual circumstances, I think, is quite lacking.

There have been some recent trends that have specifically underscored this reasoning. The elimination of Rule 390 two weeks ago, I think, will increase competition among markets and market makers and enhance more continuous trading of the most active stocks.

I also think that liquidity is another reason why our markets work so well. Although there certainly can be gaps in liquidity, I think that overall, continuous markets give investors more of an opportunity to trade when they want to and how they want to.

ECNs have allowed end users to trade directly with each other. You've heard about that earlier this morning. I know you'll hear about it again because that is caused spreads to tighten, although, we have seen certain kinds of fragmentation. Overall, I think people have more of an opportunity to trade and create more pools of liquidity than ever existed before.

Lastly, we have the boom in online trading. You cannot ignore the impact of personal computers and the ability of people to trade online. Online trading may be the most dramatic force in our markets today, for both what I'll call professional and semi-professional investors. It has also opened up access to various technologies that were previously unattainable, such as level two quotes on Nasdaq. The online revolution has certainly given online investors more of an ability to trade continuously and on more equal footing than ever before.

I will tell from you an options perspective that online trading is the biggest growth area of our business, for obvious reasons. As I said earlier, almost 40 percent of our volume is now achieved without any human intervention, meaning that we have a significant number of people trading options online at our exchange, literally, with the click of a mouse.

I would say that to switch to a call auction alone, without combining it with the continuous market, would not work at all, particularly in an environment where execution costs are falling and the speed and transparency of markets has grown dramatically.

An example of when the call auction does work very well is at the opening of the New York Stock Exchange. One of the most significant things to recognize about derivatives markets is that they are really no better than the underlying markets. If you have a very liquid underlying stock, the options are going to be liquid. Thus, if you don't have much liquidity in the underlying, the options are not going to be very liquid. I also know there can be times when there is more liquidity in the options than the underlying stock, but if the underlying stock is not very liquid, you're not going to see an active option.

One of the things we've always done in our business is wait for the underlying market to open. We do not trade the derivatives without the underlying stock opening. I'm talking about equity options. I'm not talking about index options, which are, of course, based on different things, and which have a futures component, as well. And, I'm happy to address index options in your questions, if you'd like.

In sum, I think that the opening of the New York Stock Exchange probably is the closest situation to a call auction in our markets today, and it has served us very, very well. I understand that Nasdaq is considering moving toward this model in their market opening.

An additional element that I think is important is anonymity. In this regard, the ECNs have definitely added a dimension to the liquidity of the markets; however, we're still very much dependent on the opening of the main markets as they exist today.

Now, let me turn to the options markets, and in particular, explain why I believe that the continuous market is the model that will succeed and continue to succeed in the United States.

As I previously stated, with a couple of exceptions that we've made over the years, we're very much a continuous market model. First and foremost, the keys to our markets in this country are the liquidity and transparency found here. I've traveled all over the world, visiting more stock, options and futures exchanges than anybody I know, and I've never seen the depth of liquidity that our markets maintain outside of the US, particularly if the market is not a continuous market.

Where we have succeeded in the options business in the United States – again, when I talk about the option business, I'm talking about individual equity options – has been our ability to develop new initiatives. CBOE, followed by the others, implemented the concept of continuous quoting and updating quotes in an automated fashion.

I remember my early days in the options business at the American Stock Exchange -- and I see my friend Mike Dritz in the audience -- who was one of the pioneers in those days as a specialist. When a stock would change price, the specialist would have to compute updated figures mentally and announce the price change of every option series. So, as an example, if IBM changed half a point, the specialist would say 'okay, this one is up, this one is up, this one is up; that one is down; that one is down.' It was an impossible task both mechanically and mathematically.

Over the last decade, we've developed systems like the CBOE's AutoQuote, specifically designed to handle rapid and continuous price changes efficiently. Our AutoQuote system is a very powerful force; so potent in fact, that the system creates, as I said earlier, 25 million quotes a day. That, in itself, creates its own capacity problems, but from the point of view of active markets, as the stock price moves, the option prices move in tandem. Again, you're moving a multitude of options series every time the stock moves.

Investors in the US have become very accustomed to having the ability to see a firm quote on an option or a stock that they want to be able to trade. I cannot imagine how you could do this in a call market environment. Today's options markets are too big and too complex.

Two exceptions to the continuous markets have developed. Number one, as I said, are opening procedures. When I was with the Chicago Mercantile Exchange back in 1986-87, we experienced a period when triple-witching became a really dirty word. People were very concerned that on expiration Friday, as the index futures and options expired based on the closing price of the New York Stock Exchange, that there would be wild price gyrations at the close. This was very unsettling and as the markets became more volatile in the mid-80s, there was a plea for some action to address this concern.

At the Chicago Mercantile Exchange, we addressed this issue with the NYSE by moving the settlement of the futures, and actually most of the options, to the opening of trading, rather than the close. The reason being there was no ability to have a call-type auction at the close because the close was merely the last price of the day. The last sale could be for 100 shares, or 1,000 shares, but it was very unlikely there would be 1 million shares because the specialist would be unable to slow the market down to match up buyers and sellers.

Consequently, the New York Stock Exchange on expiration Friday worked out a special kind of auction for the opening of stocks. This auction still occurs every month on expiration Friday when the specialist in the most-active stocks puts out buy and sell indications as needed. You will see enormous amounts of volume take place at the opening. If there's an imbalance, they will have a 're-indication,' and even, if necessary, delay the opening.

Undeniably, people could criticize that as holding back the opening of the markets, but if you look at the staggering level of volume that takes place on expiration Friday, a large number of shares are handled at the opening. I believe it's handled, under the circumstances, very well. I think price discovery works extremely well with this procedure in place.

From my travels to exchanges around the world, I have seen the markets outside the US experience terrific volume. However, in most cases, it's not based on continuous markets; it's more on a request for quote (RFQ) basis. I don't know what the good professor would make of this, and whether or not he would consider a request for quote is a call market. To me, it sounds more like a call market than a continuous market. I think a request for quote is fine, but it tends to work more for large, institutional investors and is not as advantageous for retail investors.

If we look at Europe, we see one exception in Amsterdam, which very much has a continuous market structure, and was, in fact, actually modeled after the CBOE in the late 70s. Otherwise, markets in Europe tend to be RFQ markets. They produce RFQ markets with tremendous volume, but a majority of it is prearranged: i.e. "meet me on the screen and here is what we're going to do." I don't view that model as benefiting investors in the same way that our options markets in the United States do today.

Market linkage is also an interesting phenomenon. The exchanges are under tremendous pressure from the SEC to link our options markets, and I believe that is a good thing. We now have four exchanges that compete in all of the most-active options. In ten days, we'll have a fifth. The question is: how does a customer know at a particular point in time that he or she is getting the best price for that option, particularly if the orders are going through these electronic systems and are routed to specific exchanges? I believe that linkage should happen, and that it should happen soon. I also feel that this is another factor that supports the concept of continuous markets over a call market.

I believe another area where continuous markets are more effective than call markets is during a stock halt. Fortunately, we don't see as many halts today as we used to because of ECNs and other competing markets to the primary markets. But, I will tell you that the absolute worst thing -- or the best way to create panic among investors -- is to stop a market. Whether you're stopping a whole market or a market for individual stock, if you don't have continuous markets, you end up with problems because people who want to get out of a position can't. The best things we as exchanges can provide for investors are transparency, liquidity and continuous markets.

We are building our own electronic trading system at CBOE, called CBOE*direct*™. It will provide for a continuous market. The system is based on the same kind of model that we have on our floor, which is an affirmative obligation to put up quotes, but I should note, we do have an RFQ feature. I think that the RFQ feature becomes very important, particularly in derivatives, when you want to do special kinds of trades, spreads or other combinations, transactions that are very different than the orders in stocks. It's also a good way to advertise that you want to do this kind of straddle or that kind of collar, or any of the other strategies that I'm sure people in this room know more about than I do these days.

In conclusion, I will wrap up, because I'd rather use the rest of my time for your questions. Our industry is in a very exciting period. We are in the midst of a technological revolution, the likes of which I have never seen. There are certainly opportunities existing for niche systems that can be created to cater to different needs of investors. Electronic systems are the way markets will be created in the future. I don't think you're going to see any more floor-based exchanges being formed. Although, I think floor-based exchanges that do exist, and ours in particular, will continue to enhance the floor with electronics. The current regulatory climate, in my opinion, is very friendly to competing systems. I sometimes think it's friendly only to our competitors and not to existing markets, but I don't want to get into that right now.

In closing, I would like to congratulate Professor Schwartz and the faculty here for doing such a great job on this symposium. The opportunity to exchange ideas is a very valuable endeavor. I thank you for the opportunity to participate today. Thank you very much.

HAROLD BRADLEY, American Century Investment Management [From the Floor]: I have a question about every form of securities market regulation.

BRODSKY: Where do you want to start?

HAROLD BRADLEY [From the Floor]: With this one. Why in the year 2000 do we, as investors, have to deal with options, futures, stocks, or other forms of securities in disparate markets? Tell me the need for separate regulatory structures and why they cannot exist uniformly on my desktop?

BRODSKY: I think you are asking two different questions: First, why are there different marketplaces? Second, why are there two different regulatory structures?

The issue of marketplaces will probably resolve itself, either through technology or regulation. I am not going to be a commercial for private vendors, but there are systems right now where you can put your information on one screen, with all of the markets you want. You can watch what you want, click, and go to the market of your choice, whether it is stocks, futures or options. I do not think it is a problem for investors if they really want to trade among different markets at the same time.

Your second question regards regulatory structure. I testified about that issue last week before a hearing of the Senate Banking Committee. I made a plea to find a way to combine the regulatory schemes of the SEC and the CFTC. We are in a regulatory backwater in the United States because we have equity products, including stocks and options and futures, regulated by two different agencies. The time has long passed where the agencies should be consolidated. If you go to any other country in the world that trades these markets, they are all under the same regulator. Quite frankly, I think our bifurcated regulatory scheme is holding back our ability to succeed.

I am leaving in 30 minutes for a plane to Washington. One of the issues I will deal with when I get to Washington today is the desire of futures exchanges to trade futures on individual stocks. Our view (and this is not just my own, but also that of the securities exchanges in the United States on whose behalf I have testified several times) is that there should be a level regulatory playing field, and that the best way to do this is to consolidate regulation.

Unfortunately, politically, it is not going to happen. So we are left with conflicts that have existed for years. I would certainly appreciate, Harold, any help you can give us in Washington.

ANDREW HOWIESON, State Street Information Partnerships [From the Floor]: The ability to put on a screen a whole collection of markets does not really do much to bring markets together. It is just putting up a TV screen with six markets on it. This does not allow an investor to actually trade simultaneously in those markets and to trade the way that he looks at a portfolio. The thrust of the question is, when are we going to use technology to produce serious linkages between markets? Somebody wanting to sell a German bund and buy a US treasury should be able to do that, without having to go to one of the big names and pay an exorbitant price to have a couple of dealers get in the middle of it.

BRODSKY: I cannot say for certain when that will occur but, having watched the pace of innovation, I will tell you that I would much prefer that the private sector rather than the government work with the markets.

These things are coming. At least in terms of my priorities, it is very important to get the options markets linked. I expect, and certainly it is my hope, that by the early part of next year, we will have quotes with size, and consolidated quotes for options, the same way stocks are currently quoted. That is the first important step. I think all of these things will come – and probably come sooner rather than later.

WILLIAM FREUND, Pace University [From the Floor]: Why do you still have a floor? Do you need the floor? Does it add to your execution costs and your competitiveness?

BRODSKY: Why do we have a floor? Because our exchange was founded with a floor.

I think there is a misconception about floor trading at exchanges versus trading in a non-floor, or electronic environment. In actuality, there is not a lot of difference between the crowd on the floor that we have trading in IBM, where everyone is using a hand-held doing trades electronically, versus going to a Morgan Stanley or a Goldman Sachs and seeing 300 people staring at computer screens. Those are trading rooms that happen to be in firms, rather than in one location.

The competitive environment we are in will determine the justification for a floor. One of the most important fundamentals of our business (and I think for all of the derivatives business) is that it may be even more important for us to have a trading floor for options than it is for the stock business. This is because of our needs – first, for liquidity, and second, to do complex trades.

In my relatively brief tenure at the CBOE (which is now three years), I have seen size and a complexity of transactions that I never would have dreamt of. Most of our business is not done on the traditional floor. It is done electronically or it is done semi-electronically.

Our job in maintaining an exchange with a floor is to make sure that the floor provides added value. If it does not have added value, it will not survive.

DAVID KRELL, International Securities Exchange [From the Floor]: Do you think that futures on stocks will become a reality and, if so, when? What implications will that have on the options markets?

BRODSKY: That is a pretty loaded question. First of all, let me refer you to this week's *Business Week*, which has a two-page spread on the subject. I think it is a matter of "when," not "if."[65] Frankly, I am very frustrated by the process because I am more concerned with the regulatory playing field — how you handle issues like insider trading, market manipulation, and suitability, as well as how you handle the margin and tax issues. An option and a future are very, very close, and yet the regulatory regimes are very different. Those issues must be resolved, as far as I am concerned, before there ever is a future on a stock.

When that time comes, will there be an impact on the options? I guess you can paint it many different ways. It depends on the users, and on the firms that support the customers. One of the things I have learned in our business is that every time you think things are bad for your business, it turns out that people dream up ways of using these new vehicles that you would have never imagined. And, overall, business grows even further.

I do not want to see the options business, with all of its safeguards and investor protections that have made it work so well over the years, be cannibalized by a business that is unequally regulated. That is my concern. All of these investment tools can work well both individually and collectively, but the problem is that we are currently under disparate regulation in this country. This has hindered our business growth against foreign competition. Because the regulatory derivatives have not been brought under one umbrella, the US has remained mired in the regulatory backwater of the world.

[65] On July 24, 2002, the SEC approved of margin requirements and other rules for single stock futures.

CHAPTER 7: INTEGRATING CALL AND CONTINUOUS TRADING[66]

Moderator – Junius Peake, *University of Northern Colorado*
Paul Davis, *TIAA-CREF*
Gerald Putnam, *Archipelago, Inc.*
Cameron Smith, *Island ECN*
Daniel Weaver, *Zicklin School of Business, Baruch College*
Steven Wunsch, *AZX, Inc.*

JUNIUS PEAKE: I started on Wall Street in 1950 at $60 a week. My first job was changing the TransLux ticker ink. I got it all over my shirt and tie, and discovered it was absolutely indelible. Wall Street, 50 years ago, was very different than it is today. We used to say that if we got paid for the quotes, we would do the executions for free, because it took you 15 minutes to find out what a quote was. We also had customers who entered orders as good until close,[67] and that was normal for them, and then they would cancel the order and move it further away from the market price.

Now to today. We have a very distinguished panel here. To introduce them, let me turn to one of my favorite books, the dictionary. We have an academician, Dan Weaver, and an academician is a member of an institution of learning. We have Gerald Putnam from Archipelago, and an Archipelago is an expanse of water with many scattered islands. Next we have Cameron Smith from Island. Is that one of the islands in the Archipelago? An island is a body of land, surrounded by water, and smaller than a continent. We have a stock exchange represented by Steven Wunsch, a stock exchange

[66] This chapter is based on the transcript of the conference, The Electronic Call Auction: New Answers to Old Questions, held at Baruch College/CUNY on May 16, 2000.

[67] Junius Peake was speaking facetiously. He was saying that when the price of a stock approached the execution price ("close" meant "near", not "at the end of the trading day"), the order would be cancelled. Peake was jokingly suggesting that when customers entered orders, they didn't really want them executed.

being a place where security trading is conducted on an organized system. And finally we have Paul Davis from TIAA-CREF.

In 1976, Morris Mendelson from the Wharton School, T. Williams and I wrote a paper.[68] In it, we talked about the fact that people were very frightened about moving to electronic trading. It was like people back in the 14th century who would draw maps of the world with pictures of sea monsters and areas labeled "terra incognito." We proposed an electronic trading system, and the proposal was turned down by everybody. The New York Stock Exchange claimed that nobody could afford an electronic trading system. It might cost as much as $20 million, they said, and where would that kind of money come from? Here we are, 25 years later. We still do not have an electronic system on the New York Stock Exchange, and they have spent $2 billion in the last few years.[69]

What we have today is dual competition for orders. We have the order that the brokerage firm wants to get from the customer. When the customer gives the order to the broker, that order, in effect, is then sold to some market center. However, what the customer wants is that the order be able to interact with every potential counter-party order.

Island ECN, in some of its recent testimony, said that it absolutely believes in price-time priority.[70] That has been one of my mantras, as well. Island does not believe in price-time priority of cross markets, however. Only within their own market can we have price-time priority. In other words, it is great in our market but no good in others.

Maybe the solution is for the SEC to do something I think they should have done 25 years ago. The Commission should issue a rule that says it wants the National Market System to operate under price-time priority. And on and after some specific date in the future, no security will trade (and be a National Market System security) unless it trades under price-time priority. We will build it. And we would build it. We would have a National Market System in a year and a half. I do not know whether Island, Archipelago, the New York Stock Exchange or Nasdaq would be the winner. But the big winners would be the customers.

[68] "Toward a Modern Exchange: The Peake, Mendelson, Williams Proposal for an Electronically-Assisted Auction Market," Morris Mendelson, Junius Peake and R. T. Williams, Jr., Reprinted in Impending Changes for Securities Markets: What Role for the Exchanges? Ernest Bloch and Robert A. Schwartz, Eds., Jai Press, Greenwich, CT 1979.

[69] The NYSE reportedly spends $400 million annually on technology, up 25% since the late 1990s. See FORTUNE magazine, April 15, 2002.

[70] See statement of Matthew Andresen, President, The Island ECN, US Senate Banking Securities Subcommittee, March 22, 2000.

I am really a continuous market fan. But I am for a call market at the opening, and possibly after the close. Maybe even in the middle of the day, if you have a hiatus. But all of those markets operate within a price-time priority system. Every single one of them. As far as I know, there is no call market that operates any differently.

So, my first question for the panel is: What is wrong with a price-time priority system which allows all of the orders to compete? One hundred percent competition. No monolith, no government saying whom the winner is. Let competition determine who wins. Who wants to take that one?

GERALD PUTMAN: I will start with an example that picks on the New York Stock Exchange. If a customer enters an order and then changes his mind because a price becomes available that would compete with the customer's order, that customer is stuck in a roach motel. If a better price occurs after you have placed your order on the NYSE, it is practically impossible to withdraw that order to try to obtain the better price. That is a problem. And this is something that we responded to across the Archipelago and Island marketplaces, and with the other ECNs. We at the ECNs get electronic responses. An order can be cancelled immediately and, unlike the NYSE, there is no manual intervention. The overhead from building a virtual limit order book among the ECNs is very small. We send the order into Island if there is a competing order there. Island gives us a very quick response; Instinet gives us a quick response. Redibook gives us a quick response.[71] We can pull an order out if the customer changes his or her mind. At the very least, Island and the others let us know immediately whether our order is executable or not. We are not suggesting that the New York Stock Exchange change its market structure. But at a minimum, for an intermarket linkage to be successful, we must be able to cancel orders, we must get an immediate quote out at the point we ask for it, not sixty seconds later.

PEAKE: Does that not support an argument for centralization? Orders that go in can be cancelled, the ones where Island goes can be cancelled?

CAMERON SMITH: Is the fundamental issue competition between markets, or competition between orders? The competition you are talking of – the essence of your argument, and correct me if I am wrong – is competition between orders. We believe that there should also be competition between markets. We have seen it in the last three years in the Nasdaq marketplace. Competition has dramatically changed the structure of that market. Competition has lowered SelectNet fees, for instance, and the facility is providing much better service than it did three years earlier.

[71] Redibook and Archipelago have since merged.

PEAKE: If I were to ask you, what is the market in AT&T, are you going to tell me that it is Island's bid, offered at Archipelago, or are you going to give me two numbers?

SMITH: I would want to use a Nasdaq stock, not an NYSE stock, in your analogy. As you know, we do not currently trade listed stocks on Island. And, due to some regulatory barriers, neither does Archipelago.

PEAKE: What is a market? Is a market a price or a place? I say it is a price.

GERALD PUTNAM: "Place" is thinking in terms of geography. When you start talking about moving bids around the globe, maybe we don't have to think about place anymore.

PEAKE: Two different lines on a screen are in different places. If the broker who was given the order was not a member of the NYSE, and the NYSE had the best price, the broker would either have to execute the order elsewhere (at an inferior price), or redirect it to a member. Can you interact if I am not a member of the New York Stock Exchange, and I send an order to Island for execution?

SMITH: No. Again, this is because we have not benefited from inclusion in the listed market systems. Let's say we had an IBM order and that it was not the best price. The order has no visibility to the wider investing public because, unlike in Nasdaq where visibility is required by the order handling rules, that requirement was not placed on an unlisted market such as Island. So, we have no visibility of quotes, and you do not know we have a quote there. Secondly, you have no linkage to us.

PEAKE: Paul Davis, where do you decide to send your orders when you have got 200 billion to work?

PAUL DAVIS: We have a number of portfolio management strategies, and the one we use dictates how we trade an order. One easy way to view the problem is, simply, in terms of small, medium and large trades.

You have got to deal with those different kinds of orders differently. We have one strategy that enables us, essentially, to pretend to be a retail trader. That is, we can break an order up and trade it in small pieces (we do it this way on the ECNs). We are connected directly to SuperDot and can participate electronically all day long, conducting thousands of trades.

Let us look at a large order. How do you really execute a large piece of business? The way markets are structured today it is very, very difficult. It has become extremely costly. We have a better handle on trading costs now than we did five years ago. Five years ago, I was not measuring the costs of this kind of trading. But we have a pretty good sense that it is very, very expensive. We need market structures that will support the large orders. We need efficient trading of large orders.

I am a little disappointed to hear that, in Paris, the calls are doing only about seven percent of the business. I am a proponent of call markets. We get a lot of our business done in call markets.[72] I would like to see calls be a viable part of the Nasdaq marketplace. We get a lot of our business done on the New York open.

We are thinking in naive ways of using automation. There are some marvelous opportunities out there. Just to mention one, there is an idea that a virtual crowd could support almost any kind of trading activity. The door is open for designing virtual crowds that could support continuous trading, or that that could support call auctions.

I hope that people will start opening those doors. I hope they will think about those structures that would support large institutions as well as the retail business. Right now, all the focus seems to be on retail.

STEVEN WUNSCH: That is where it is. On retail business.

PEAKE: Steve Wunsch, any comments?

WUNSCH: I am nervous about mandates. Mandates, such as price-time priority for cross markets, may sound fair. And they may be efficient if you are thinking about the market in AT&T or in any other individual stock. But price-time priority eliminates the ability of individual markets to distinguish themselves by providing a particular kind of time and price priority, or a certain type of order-handling treatment that may be required to attract, for example, Paul Davis' large orders. I run a call market. I may not want to have the exact same kind of time and price priority that you might try to mandate from on high.

If, for example, you want a call to be transparent, you have to make time priority more important than price priority, so that it becomes time/price, rather than price/time priority. If you do not do that, then people will use the information in the open, transparent book to step ahead of orders. The problem is exacerbated in a decimal environment, where you could take a trade away from a large order that got there first by just stepping ahead of it by a penny. If you put price ahead of time in your priority scheme, then no one would be foolish enough to put orders out in the open, and you would not have an open book anymore.

So, while I think that price and time priorities are generally the right kind of priorities, we at AZX have put a greater emphasis on time than on price. Other systems, with different concerns, might do things differently. Bill Lupien's system, for example, does not require time priority because OptiMark does not have an open book. OptiMark is a sealed-bid-type

[72] Paul Davis explained later that his firm, TIAA-CREF executes orders through arrangements with broker-dealers. In any instances, orders for TIAA-CREF are traded on NYSE's 'call' at the open.

system with rapid-fire calls. This illustrates that different types of structures can evolve when systems have the freedom to design their own rules and priorities. But if you have any specific priority system mandated from on high, you will not have the beneficial market structure competition that we all seem to want.

PEAKE: I teach a course in market microstructure every fall, and I never have to buy a textbook. The SEC writes it for me. Every year, the Commission comes out with a new release correcting, in great detail, the mistakes it made the previous year. For eight years, I never failed to get a 200-page release, which I would ask the students to go through. We would walk our way through it and, at the end, the students would throw up their hands and say, "Can you believe these people are being ordered to do that?"

Are you suggesting, Steve, that the SEC presently *should not* have any rules, and that price-time priority would somehow be more awful than the millions of rules that have been introduced and then amended?

WUNSCH: I agree with Doug Atkin's comment earlier that we all have regulatory fatigue at this point. The SEC attempts constantly to correct last year's mistakes. This happens with one mandatory rule that all markets are going to have to adhere to. If we get where the SEC is trying to take us, we will have in effect linked everything together and turned everything into a single market. I know that is something you NMS aficionados want. I know that you may not be concerned if that single market mandates out of the picture such things as call markets, or such things as any unique order handling processes that an Island or an Archipelago might want to introduce for their specific types of customers. I believe that customers should be free to use or not use any markets that do or do not suit them. I do not see why all types of markets cannot compete for their business, as well as interact with and work with each other without mandates.

For example, our call market can operate during the day, or at the open, or at the close, entirely independently of what is happening in the continuous market. You do not need to mandate common order handling rules across all markets. If you do, in fact, you will kill that opportunity.

DANIEL WEAVER: Price-time priority is not necessarily a good thing overall. I think that if a market chooses to have price-time priority within its own system, that is wonderful. I believe more along the lines of what the New York Stock Exchange has come up with recently – namely, full disclosure, letting people know the parameters of a particular market.

I used to be an advocate of strict price-time priority. However, with adherence to price-time priority, you negate the supposed benefit of price improvement. I like price improvement much better, don't you?

PEAKE: I say price improvement is a fraud. It does not exist. At the time of execution, somebody has to know what the highest bid and lowest offer is. The problem we have today is that the systems in place (and approved by the SEC) do not require that all market participants have equal access to the best bid and offer. When a subset has information not available to the rest of the potential buyers and sellers, they claim price improvement. But the NBBO[73] does not always contain the highest bids and lowest offers. But, keep going, Dan.

WEAVER: An NYSE specialist will take a market order and a limit order and wait for an incoming market order to cross it, and cross the two market orders in the middle. With price-time priority, you cannot have that kind of interaction. You can argue that it is a fraud, but when I have gotten price improvement, I have liked it. Investors should be allowed to direct their orders to the exchange that gives them the characteristics they are looking for. I think that is what we should have in the US

PEAKE: What you are suggesting is that I should not do business with Solomon or Merrill Lynch. I should do business with the New York Stock Exchange, Archipelago or Island. Are you saying that the only people I should deal with are those with the orders that we want, and to have rules that require them to execute these orders? In other words, if I send my order to Merrill Lynch, I do not decide where that order is going. Merrill decides where that order is going. I do not have any control over where my order is executed. Merrill does it. I am not knocking Merrill or picking on it for any reason, but it is doing it in Merrill's best interest, which may or may not be in my best interest. So that is your recommendation? Go to the market and not to the broker-dealer?

WEAVER: Investors ought to take more charge of where their orders are directed. The growth of the Internet is allowing investors to have access to real-time quotes, so they can see where the best prices are. Coupling that knowledge with information about the quality of execution at a venue, allows investors to make intelligent order routing decisions.

WUNSCH: That is definitely where the market is going. You see more and more investors receiving real-time quotes over the Web. Investors have access to information they never had before. Brokers are increasingly accountable for the quality of their executions, to the extent that they are sending them to markets that are affiliates of their firms. That is why they send them the order. I have a lot of faith that investors are going to understand execution quality better as the years go by. In the end, the

[73] National Best Bid or Offer (NBBO) refers to the single highest bid price from among all bids quoted by the various participants (stock exchange specialists and third market dealers) in the Consolidated Quotation Service and the single lowest offer price from among all offers quoted by those participants.

markets that please the customers will be able to gather order flow, and we will not have to mandate anything.

ROBERT SCHWARTZ, Baruch College [From the Floor]: Jay, are you thinking primarily of retail customers or of institutional customers?

PEAKE: I will answer in two parts. First, institutional investors represent individual retail investors.

ROBERT SCHWARTZ [From the Floor]: That is not my question. Consider an institutional order, like a Paul Davis order. I know he has my pension fund and he probably has yours, too. The fact is, he has an order that he is bringing to the market.

PEAKE: I was trying to suggest first that the ultimate consumer is the individual, and that institutions aggregate individual orders. But the answer is the same as Doug Atkin gave earlier. You have got to treat everybody equally. If they want to change the Securities Exchange Act of 1934, fine. If they want to change Section 8, great, change it. But the way the law is written today, you must provide equal information about markets.

If you are on the floor of the New York Stock Exchange and happen to know the specialist who has your order, and he gets a market order, does somebody out in San Francisco on the Pacific Exchange know anything about this? No. There is no possibility of that in the present system. Everybody would like to get the best possible price. The only point of best execution is that the buyer wants to pay the least total cost, and the seller wants to get the most proceeds, period. There is no such thing as price improvement if you know the best prices that are being offered. If you know that you have access to all bids and offers. There is no other way to do it. The question is, do you see all bids and offers?

WEAVER: But Jay, you are requiring everyone to display all of their liquidity. You cannot force investors to display the liquidity. If you try to do that, they are only going to pocket it.

PEAKE: Ok, on the floor of the New York Stock Exchange, does an undeclared bid or offer have any standing? No. I rest my case.

DAVIS: I would like to comment on that. I think that Bob's little Economics 101 presentation this morning was a good one. It is not just price discovery that we are talking about. Throughout all of this, we are talking about price discovery and quantity discovery. Quantity discovery is so very important for the large orders. With a large order, I know that I am going to be paying out to get it executed. I am quite willing to pay up for that. The important thing is to get the quantity done.

PEAKE: But when you pay up for it, should the seller of the 100 shares who entered the best price, get an execution?

DAVIS: If it is a central marketplace that I am dealing in and I have to clear those 100 shares, and I am happy to do it. It does not have to be that way, though.

PEAKE: Why not? Because the little guy needs to be taken care of as much as the big guy, I think.

DAVIS: In our case, two million little guys.

PEAKE: Should the one 100-share guy be told that you were the first, that you created the price, and the heck with you? We are going to give it to two million other people because your order was only for 100 shares and mine was for 2 million? That is not fair. Best bid, first entered, and best offer, first entered (regardless of size) should be first executed. First-come, first-served is the time honored American measure of fairness.

PUTNAM: This whole argument leads to the conclusion that competition is good. And I will disagree with what you said earlier, that there will be a winner. Today, in the options marketplace, there is not a winner. There are four exchanges. We compete with one another. There is one that is bigger than the rest,[74] but they all exist with their own value propositions. It has made those marketplaces better. If we were to decide on a winner, or to set up a framework where there could be a winner, I think people would be at a disadvantage under your argument. You might be an investor who wants to send an order to one marketplace, let us say to OptiMark. You get a large order executed at a price that fits your needs. That is great. Maybe our marketplace, or the Island marketplace, is where individuals get time and price priority. Perhaps those two marketplaces try to link up to one another and share their liquidity. That is a better outcome than setting up a system for a single marketplace, which becomes a monopoly.

PEAKE: You don't have to anoint a winner. Competition will do it. A market system is a natural monopoly. How about our academician here, Dan Weaver? Are these natural monopolies? If you have one market that is attracting all of the business because it is the best in a stock, is it a natural monopoly?

WEAVER: Yes, it would be. But I would like to talk about something else.

I heard a lot this morning about call markets versus continuous markets. I had the distinct impression, listening to the speakers, that all stocks should be treated the same way. I do not agree. For example, if you take a look at the New York Stock Exchange, the specialist makes the market on both

[74] There are five US options exchanges, the Chicago Board Options Exchange (CBOE), the American Stock Exchange, the International Securities Exchange, the Pacific Coast Exchange, and the Philadelphia Stock Exchange. The largest of these is the CBOE.

sides in really illiquid stocks and limit orders make up the market for the more liquid issues. We should come back to what we are supposed to be talking about, integrating call markets and continuous markets. Call markets on some stocks will be more important than on other stocks.

Returning to the airplane analogy we used this morning, continuous markets would seem to be the only way to go, because investors want immediate gratification. But let us talk again about airlines. How many of you were ever on an overbooked flight? If they announced the flight was overbooked, and they would like people to volunteer to get off the flight, offering a free ticket on the next flight out plus two dollars to encourage them nobody would go for it. But if they made it a $500 voucher, it would become economically efficient for people to volunteer. Alternatively stated, in the call market context, if people got a sufficiently better deal by waiting for a call, they would wait. They would dispense with "immediate execution."

I think that this is what we need to do with call markets in general, and OptiMark in particular. The economic need for OptiMark is in illiquid stocks which typically have wide spreads. Then it becomes attractive for traders to trade inside the spread or to have liquidity accumulated.

We should drop the notion that we should have one system for all stocks. For illiquid stocks, call markets make a lot of sense. For the IBM's and AT&T's, let us do continuous trading.

PEAKE: But you are proposing price-time priority for both systems, no? Using your airline analogy, would you like to have competing air traffic controllers at the same airport? If you are for competition, why do you want just one? That is a monopoly, and that is bad.

WEAVER: I am saying we should merge together different trading systems.

WUNSCH: We should have multiple types of markets. We also do not want to have to pick one for small stocks, and another for big stocks. Let the public choose for all stocks.

Bill Brodsky in his talk spoke about how, in the old days, there were call markets, and then everyone graduated to continuous markets, as if it were a natural evolution. I suppose it exposes his bias. Is he worried that we might all switch back to the call markets? Certainly, Dan Weaver is not advocating that, and neither would I. You certainly would have continuous markets operating if the markets went to seven days a week, and you could still have call markets at certain points in time. Having them less frequently than two or three times a day may be adequate. It may be enough to get the full impact of what a call market can bring.

PEAKE: I have no quarrel with that. But let me ask, why is it that, if the New York Stock Exchange is the best system there is, no one has copied its design? Can anyone answer that question? Assuming that it is the best system?

WEAVER: Toronto and Amsterdam have copied the NYSE.

PEAKE: Do they have specialists?

WEAVER: Yes.

PEAKE: Do they have a floor in Toronto?

WEAVER: They did away with it.

ALLAN GRODY, Financial InterGroup Holdings [From the Floor]: The New York Stock Exchange has not been copied because it has a unique history and tradition that is associated with the American spirit of risk-taking and diverse culture. And it has been working.

DAVIS: Why has no one copied the New York Stock exchange? I will try to speak to that in terms of the large orders that I referred to before. We recently did a $600 million trade, mainly on the NYSE floor, and the result was very good. I am happy that it was a New York Stock Exchange stock. I am happy because intermediaries could negotiate and do the tranches of the trade over time, and that they could get it done for us at reasonable prices. It would have been much more difficult on Nasdaq. I would have hesitated to do it on Nasdaq. In general, it is also much more difficult to do trades like this $600 million one if your market structure is restricted – as it is in many of the European countries – to an order-driven market that is primarily for retail orders. I would not want to break that order up into a gazillion little pieces that would have to be worked over time in this type of market. There are times when the New York Stock Exchange serves us very, very well.

ROBERT SCHWARTZ [From the Floor]: What I have been hearing is that there are problems in working big institutional orders. We heard it in the first panel. We hear it all the time. Institutions break up their orders. They feed them into the market over extended periods. I see the call market as a solution to the problems faced by institutional investors. I have heard a lot of experts echoing that view. A call is of interest to the institutions, and they are willing to wait for calls. A call could also have important implications for retail customers.

It is not difficult to integrate the call and continuous markets if you use the call as an opening procedure. What if we were to pick a different time, perhaps have a call at 12 noon? Could we do it? Would it be helpful to the institutions? How would you integrate it with the continuous market? I would like to direct that question to Steve Wunsch.

WUNSCH: First, it is possible, and even desirable, to have something that does not shut down continuous trading. There is no reason to shut down continuous trading in order to have a call market. There are different order types and different ways to treat them. You can have a call market at noon while there is a continuous market operating. Furthermore, this market would work with very large orders and with 100 share retail orders or less. You can have everybody get the same price and time priorities.

SMITH: Sorry to interrupt, but how do you do price discovery in that 12 noon auction? Is it a derivative price?

WUNSCH: No. You take in limit orders and call market orders, and you can accommodate other orders from the continuous market only if they are directed to the call market and get the call market treatment. You cannot get your order effectively time-stamped for time priority purposes until you place it in the call. That can be done at the last second, or at any time when the order placer wants to step into the queue to get time priority in the call market.

In answer to Jay Peake's question, if there were ten different call markets operating at noon, pretty quickly you would find out which one people wanted to use.

PEAKE: Say there was one at 11:15, 11:27, 11:42 --

WUNSCH: Competition will solve that, too, because calls will not be run successfully every two minutes, or every 15 minutes, in my judgment. They will be run more like every two to four hours, or else they will cannibalize each other. A good call at noon will not only kill off any other good call at noon. It will also kill off any other call at 12:30 or 11:30 or 1:00.

PEAKE: Suppose I am a broker, and that I get a limit order from a customer to buy 100 shares at 20, and that I put that order in for the 12 o'clock call. Suppose that, in the continuous market just preceding the noon call, the stock trades at 19 ¾, and that in the call it trades at 20. My customer will say, gee you could have bought the shares for me two seconds ago and saved me a quarter of a point. What the heck did you stick it in the call for? Somebody is going to be a winner and somebody is going to be a loser if the prices are different.

WUNSCH: You have to educate the consumer. If he wants the continuous price and wants to pay the liquidity spread for continuous trading, he will do that. If he wants to get the common price created in the noon call, then he may want to forgo the continuous price because, on average, he will get a better price by waiting for the call.

PEAKE: I can drown in a lake with an average depth of three feet, too, if I happen to be in the twenty-foot end. The average trader is not trading thousands of shares all day long. I make one trade on a call market. If I find out that I am paying a quarter or half a point too much, that I could have paid less on a continuous market, I am going to complain about it. After I am told it is an average price. Giving people an average price all the time will not make them happy if they could have done better elsewhere under a different system.

DAVIS: Any marketplace is governed by a set of rules. I happened to bring along a fact book on the Tokyo Stock Exchange. It has a market structure that parallels some of these issues quite nicely. For those of you who are not familiar with the structure in Tokyo, they open their morning session with a call market, they trade continuously for two hours, they close with a call market, and then they have a nice, leisurely lunch. They come back, open their afternoon session with a call market, trade for two more hours in a continuous market, and then close with another call.

Two interesting facts. One, the Tokyo system has been in place since 1967. So people seem to be able to say, okay, that is a pretty good set of rules. I think that we can play the game with this set of rules. The other thing I found interesting – nowhere in the book do they mention having call auctions. I asked them about that, and they looked at me as if to say, is there any other way to open or to close a continuous market? It is a different set of rules, and it is working very well.

PEAKE: Have you counted the number of lawyers in Japan versus the number of lawyers in the United States? I am sorry to be facetious, but I think you know where I am coming from. I am suggesting that the Japanese are much more ready to accept market (and other) rules than Americans. We are the most litigious society in the world!

WILLIAM HARTS, Nasdaq [From the Floor]: Let us say that you give an order to your broker, and either agree or ask him to place that order in a 12 noon cross. Then the price that you paid for those 100,000 shares was a dollar higher than the quoted price on the New York Stock Exchange. Would you not have a difficult conversation with the sales trader at that point? Would you be okay with that price?

DAVIS: If I got 100,000 shares done at a dollar higher? It really depends on the liquidity of the stock. It could be a very good trade.

WILLIAM HARTS [From the Floor]: Is disclosure the key, or would you want to make the decision as to whether you would go into the cross at all? Would it be enough for the broker to say to you, we intend to put your order into the 12-noon auction?

DAVIS: I would encourage my broker to use a 12-noon auction if there was one. I do not know if you have had the luxury of using the software that is available in the Subotnick Financial Services Center here at Baruch College, but it is interesting. Bob Schwartz and Bruce Weber have designed a trading simulation that includes several different market structures. Try the scenario with a call market embedded in a continuous market structure, and you will find out that you trade quite differently. You can really be cute in the continuous market, and trade to get some stuff done. If you do not seem to be getting it done, you know you can be aggressive in the call market and at least get your fill.

There are lots of ways to use a call market structure. We are talking about a hybrid market structure, and about having calls as part of the market structure.

PUTNAM: Paul Davis could put that order in himself today. If he did, he would not have to ask a broker if he got a price that was inferior or superior.[75] Do what on-line traders do on the Internet every day. Just do it yourself. You have direct access.

MIKE DRITZ, Dritz Enterprises [From the Floor]: Tradescpae.com provides what you may be looking for.[76] You said you could get an order in without selecting where you want it to go for your broker. Today, there is transparency, there is visibility, and they have provided a mechanism for customers to make a selection. Our customers and other on-line day trading firms now have the ability to hit a heat-seeking button, which picks the best market, and gives you the linkage you are looking for. Alternatively, the customers can select an individual market because there may be latent demand and size and other questions.

ECNs have spawned a new industry. As a result, there are hundreds of thousands of transactions going through these systems. This has increased the volume on Nasdaq much more appreciably than in New York Stock Exchange stocks.[77] This competition has created a fantastic marketplace. It has helped to tighten spreads, and reduced the cost so that people can trade just like the professionals trade.

PEAKE: Why would somebody want to send their order to A, B, C, or D market when you can offer them the best market?

MIKE DRITZ [From the Floor]: There are lots of reasons. For example, if you talk about latency, at any particular time during any particular day, one of the ECNs may be operating in executions of milliseconds, and the others may be operating in five or ten second speeds. If you are an active trader, it may be more important for you to go to one particular system because you know you will get a quicker execution. If you go to another

[75] At a conference at Baruch College in June 2002, Paul Davis made a reference to the cost of his firm establishing its own direct execution services, compared with it current arrangements using the intermediation and network services of NYSE member broker-dealers. It was not clear to him at this 2002 conference if it would be cost-effective for TIAA to have its own brokerage services. Therefore, he still continues to "ask a broker if he got a price that was inferior or superior."

[76] Tradescape is a provider of trading software that gives the individual investor on line access to the stock market, avoiding middlemen.

[77] Nasdaq volume on ECNs continued to rise since the 2000 conference. By early 2002, ECNs handled up to 50% of Nasdaq trade volume compared with about 7% of trade volume in NYSE stocks in electronic marketplaces.

system offering the best bid and offer, it might take you two more seconds and you could miss the execution. What Tradescape does is it gives you a choice.

PEAKE: So, each of them has a little notice stating, "we're on a five second delay," "we're on a nine-second delay," "we're on a two-second delay," and you just pick one?

MIKE DRITZ [From the Floor]: Yes, that is one of a dozen criteria on our screen.

WEAVER: When you say best market, you are saying best price, right? There are plenty of other reasons for what might make it best for me: more liquidity, more speed, but you are assuming its price?

PEAKE: You may trade in 50,000 share blocks, but wouldn't you want to make sure to pay the lowest total cost for each execution, the moment you make that trade or bid, and receive the greatest amount of proceeds if a sale?

WEAVER: If you get the best price at any one point in time, but you have 100,000 or a million shares to do, it could happen that you get a lousy price for the whole block. If the whole system is only designed to get a best price, at an instant in time, with many of those orders sequentially lined up, you could get killed.

PEAKE: But if I decide that I am going to put in 50,000, I want the best price for my 50,000.

WUNSCH: 50,000 is way too big in today's market.

HAROLD BRADLEY, American Century Investment Management [From the Floor]: I used to manage a million dollar portfolio of mid-cap growth companies. When I was worried about a stock, I would look at what was trading in the market, because we did not have an effective block-clearing mechanism. I put 50,000 shares out there, or 100,000 knowing full well that I had a million shares to sell.

You would give the order to your trader and it goes to his floor, and he calls the sales trader in Chicago, who calls the position trader in New York, who calls the floor broker on the floor of the NYSE. Then it goes into the crowd and the specialist is told that he has 25,000 for sale with more to follow. Where is it going to open? Then the calls come back up the chute. I have only put in a quarter of what I want to get done by the time all of my seven agents have helped me, and the stock moves a half point anyway, and all of the calls go back up the line to say, do you want to do more or less?

A call market allows me to reveal my true intentions at an appropriate price, and to clear without having to worry about information leakage along the way, as I proceed along on a path surrounded by seven wolves who just want to eat a little bit of Little Red Riding Hood.

PEAKE: I have no problem with calls, as long as they have price-time priority along with everything else.

SMITH: One of your basic assumptions is that all of these prices are accessible. Unfortunately, as we know too well in Nasdaq, and also with New York Stock Exchange prices, just because a quote is there, does not necessarily mean that you will get an execution. You are assuming instantaneous executions. Unfortunately, we do not live in that world. It goes back to the competition between markets. If we are all linked instantaneously, how do you differentiate markets?

PEAKE: You have to have a single queue. There is no other way to do it.

PUTNAM: What happens when the queue breaks? It breaks in Nasdaq on a regular basis, on the SelectNet system, it breaks.[78]

PEAKE: I've seen the NYSE shut down for days. The world does not come to an end.

PUTNAM: Well, it does come to an end for continuous trading. All I am saying is competing linkages and competing market places will allow for multiple linkages.

PEAKE: If you put this complex together you have got a lot more chance for breakage than if you build a clean system.

PUTNAM: No, it is like the Internet today. If AT&T controlled the Internet and it broke, it would be broken. But today MCI is there, and Sprint, and everyone else is in there to rely on. You do not have a single point of failure. Our customers use multiple linkages just in case of that.

PEAKE: I do not disagree with you, except that when the New York Stock Exchange closes down because they have a fire in their telephone system. I do not think there is going to be much trading going on on listed stocks.

PUTNAM: I did not start the fire.

PEAKE: Integrating call markets and continuous markets is important. The two can co-exist. But they really should be integrated within the same mechanism, per security. You could have competition among securities. You could have one market that trades inactive stocks with price-time priority. Another might not want the inactives but will accept the large cap stocks. Whatever the system, you really want to have 100 percent of the order flow because this way it does not cost anything to get access to it. Where does that order flow come from today? Not directly from your customers who are paying a commission. But it comes from other brokers under payment for order flow arrangements.

[78] SuperSOES is reportedly improving overall Nasdaq network performance while reducing the kind of problems cited by the speaker in Nasdaq dealer trading.

KALMAN COHEN, Duke University [From the Floor]: Steve Wunsch, what if your Arizona Stock Exchange did have a price discovery call, say at 12 noon, on continuously traded stocks, while continuous trading is in process. I do not see why it would be a problem if the world knew that at 11:55 a.m. trading in a stock on the continuous market would, by mandate, stop for five minutes and reopen with a call at 12 noon. After the call, the market would resume in the continuous trading mode. You would avoid a lot of problems about who wants to trade and in what form, and they would not be out of sequence prices. So what would be the problem if one wanted to have a noon crossing, if everybody knew in advance that it would occur five minutes beforehand? Sort of like the Tokyo Exchange right now, where a call closes the morning session. Nobody is shocked because it is a predetermined close.

WUNSCH: There is no reason to close the continuous market, other than what you mentioned, namely, the out of sequence prices. But with the out of sequence prices, people understand that the call could be a large number of people getting together, some with large orders, and some with small orders. The large number of people would be getting together to find a call market price, in a call market context, with the call market order handling priorities. They would be doing it at the same time as continuous trading is going on. That is not really a problem for either operation, the continuous or the call. I do not see any reason to deny those who would want to trade continuously, and not participate in the call, the opportunity to do so while we are having the call.

Another reason to have the call and continuous markets operate simultaneously is that you then have what I would call a "natural circuit breaker" that is always in operation. You do not have to shut the markets down in order for the circuit breaker to work its wonders. If the market starts to get unruly or volatile, people will tend to withdraw from continuous trading, the costs of which will rise in favor of the call. Directing more orders into the call will have a dampening effect on volatility.

So, the best of all worlds is to have both calls at specific times, and continuous running markets all the time. The problem is that, when you have no calls operating with any meaningful price discovery effect, you can get into significant volatility that needs the market to be shut down. And they still do not know how to set up a good call to reopen the market.

But both in very volatile times and in normal times, I see no reason why you cannot allow the call and continuous trading to operate simultaneously.

WILLIAM LUPIEN, OptiMark [From the Floor]: That is what is going to happen with OptiMark and Archipelago. OptiMark will allow the call market to take a snapshot of the continuous market and actually include orders in the continuous market in the call clearing price. Computers are doing this so fast, it is in milliseconds. It is not the same thing as holding the call auction and then turning back to the floor to see if there are any other prices that are scattering in.

PEAKE: In the interest of full disclosure, I should tell you that I am a very small shareholder of OptiMark. So I am glad to hear what you are saying.

I would like to ask each of the panel members to answer three questions. If the first question is answered yes, you do not have to answer the other two. The first question: Do we today have the National Market System that Congress asked for in 1975? Second, if your answer is anything other than an absolute yes, where will the National Market System be this time next year? The last question, which is the most important, is, will we ever see a National Market System? Paul Davis, what do you think?

DAVIS: We did not know in 1975 what a national market was going to look like in the year 2000. And so I will say that what we have now is a National Market System.

PUTNAM: I say no. The element of competition is not there. The rules that were written to put ITS and other exchange clubs in place are not open enough to allow for competition. A year from now, hopefully, we will be closer to a National Market System.[79]

PEAKE: Third question. Will we ever have a National Market System?

PUTNAM: Yes, I believe that we will.

PEAKE: Will we ever see one, you and I?

PUTNAM: Yes, we will.

PEAKE: How old will you be?

PUTNAM: It is coming now. Things are moving quickly. It will be here sooner than you think.

SMITH: I agree with Jerry Putnam, I think the answer to your first question is "no." Two of the main goals of the National Market System were to promote competition among markets and to increase the amount of quotation information available to investors. Ironically, as we sit here today, twenty-five years later, the National Market System structures -- meaning,

[79] In follow-up remarks in June 2002, Putnam noted that Archipelago has since launched the Archipelago Exchange (ArcaEx), which allows Archipelago to more directly represent its listed stock quotes in the Intermarket Trading System. ITS connects the NYSE, the regional exchanges, Nasdaq as well as ArcaEx, enabling the routing of listed stock quotes among participants. Putnam cites this as evidence that the US equity markets are moving a step closer to the congressional vision of a National Market System. ArcaEx also operates two single price Dutch auctions daily during the market pre-opening hours: 8 a.m. for limit orders; 9.30 a.m. for market and unexecuted limit orders.

the Intermarket Trading System, the Consolidated Quote System[80]-- are inhibiting those two very things in the listed market. To the extent that Archipelago or Island has a better quote on a NYSE listed stock for, let us say, AOL, no one is going to see that information. Consequently, we are really denied the ability to compete for that order flow effectively. In a year's time, that impediment may be removed when ECNs are allowed to reflect their quotes in a consolidated quotation system, and can attract flow and truly compete with the New York Stock Exchange.[81]

WEAVER: The answer is no, and where we are going to be a year from now depends on the SEC. If the SEC drops their mantra about looking for the best price, and we have to worry about liquidity as well, we will be much closer to a National Market System. If not, we will be much further away than we are right now.

WUNSCH: This is the toughest question of all. I think the National Market System is in the eye of the beholder. The SEC uses it that way. So does every rent-seeking participant in the marketplace. Unfortunately, we do have, say, 90 percent of the National Market System as it could possibly be implemented. We may get to 100 percent, which I would say is probably a full CLOB, or something like that. But it would be disastrous if we do. It would lead us even further down the road we have been going down, to less liquidity and more volatility. The whole thing should be repealed before it leads to

[80] The Consolidated Quote System is a computerized system that collects and disseminates, electronically, current bid and ask quotations along with volume, from and to all market centers trading listed stocks.

[81] Smith was referring to the applications for securities exchange status filed with the SEC by Island and Archipelago ECNs. While Archipelago's application was successful, Island's is still officially pending, as of July 2002. Exchange status, as mentioned in earlier footnote, opens a direct link to the Intermarket Trading System. It also opens a direct link to the National Consolidated Quote System. The latter system broadcasts members' best prices in listed stocks.

another market collapse that will make '87 – or even '29 -- look like a picnic.

PEAKE: We will have to leave it on that note. It has been an exciting panel. Thank you.

CHAPTER 8: A CALL AUCTION'S ROLE IN THE MARKETPLACE[82]

Robert Wood, *University of Memphis*
Kim Bang, *Bloomberg Tradebook*
Harold S. Bradley, *American Century Investment Management*
William G. Christie, *Vanderbilt University*
Peter Jenkins, *Deutsche Bank*[83]
George Sofianos, *Goldman Sachs, Inc.*[84]
Benn Steil, *Council on Foreign Relations*

ROBERT WOOD: Harold Bradley was one of the first buyside traders to realize that he could buy at the bid or sell at the offer by placing limit orders rather than market orders. He was one of the first to realize that he could supply liquidity rather than demand it. He could earn that bid/ask spread rather than pay for it. His venue for doing this was Instinet, when it became an anonymous system in the late 1980s. Harold, I want to start by asking you why others are not taking advantage of this kind of opportunity.

HAROLD BRADLEY: That is a difficult question. One of the big problems in this industry relates to soft dollars.[85] The SEC should look far more closely at soft dollar practices, and scrutinize how commission dollars are spent.

[82] This chapter is based on the transcript of the conference, The Electronic Call Auction: New Answers to Old Questions, held at Baruch College/CUNY on May 16, 2000.

[83] At the time of the conference, Peter Jenkins was with Scudder Kemper Investments. On April 8, 2002, Scudder was acquired by Deutsche Bank.

[84] At the time of the conference, George Sofianos was Vice President, International and Research at the New York Stock Exchange.

[85] "Soft dollars" refers to payments to a full-service brokerage for its services in terms of commission revenue, rather than actual cash payments. Also see footnote 10.

If you look at trading volume from 1989 to this date, according to data calculated by SEI,[86] the average commission rate has stayed pretty constant every year for institutions at about 8.5 cents a share, while volume has gone up eight or nine times. I am not an economist, but isn't it reasonable to expect, if we had a ten-fold increase in volume, that prices would go down a little bit?

This is the only market where you can split a stock, charge the same commission per share and, thereby, make more money.[87] The buyside does not have to be accountable for how they spend it. Best execution is some big cloud up there that we all recognize when we see it, but that we only pay lip service to. However, the cost comes right out of the performance line.

WOOD: Currently, there seems to be a preference for a crossing mechanism at the midpoint, rather than a call. Why are calls not used more?

PETER JENKINS: It is simple. There is a fear about discovering price. It is much easier, as it was said earlier today, to do a VWAP order, than to discover price. That is the problem with OptiMark and AZX. If you are not willing to discover price, and really buy volume at a price, you are not going to be able to participate in a price discovery call.

BRADLEY: There is another reason. An institutional order can be entered into a call market without a broker. But we institutional traders as a group like to use a broker. With a broker, you always have somebody to blame. As a former trader and portfolio manager, I know that most traders want somebody to blame because most portfolio managers do not understand how things really work.

JENKINS: The broker's side has created tools. We heard of a new type of order today that I have never heard of before – a resting market order.[88]

[86] SEI, a trade consulting service owned by CRA Associates in Chicago, uses the Gil Beebower methodology that evaluated a trade's cost by comparing the trade's day after performance to the market and the industry group. American Century, where Harold Bradley has worked variously as a head trader, portfolio manager and in other senior positions, has used the same data source for 15 years.

[87] Harold Bradley explained later that he was implying that commission costs were fixed at 6 cents a share. Otherwise, he contended, scale economics would suggest that the ten-fold increase in trading volume should have produced some price competition in commissions. Data indicate it hasn't. In a corollary argument, he said, only in the US stock market can one "split" a whole into two and then charge twice as much for the same unit of value, as happens in a stock split. Bradley also noted that in Europe, commissions are assessed as a percent of principal traded. In other words, stocks wouldn't be split so much in the US if the US markets followed the European example, charging commissions as a percent of principal.

[88] Resting market orders are given by clients and are constrained to trade only if a block of some size trades at the same time.

There is always a new type of order to create an excuse, as Harold Bradley said.

From the retail perspective, you have the wholesalers providing payment for order flow. Does anybody really look at what actually happens to the order? What percentage of those orders are resting market orders? How much is a dealer making on those resting market orders? Obviously not a lot, because he would not be a huge participant in the marketplace. It is not the same issue with the buyside. There is another order that is created on the floor of the exchange, a go-along order. I hear about orders sent to floor brokers that are ridiculous. They are not discovering price. They are copping out of their job. Their real job is to discover price, and to find the liquidity.

ROBERT SCHWARTZ [From the Floor]: You are right about nobody individually wanting to take responsibility for price discovery, and neither should they. But, if you have a call auction with a critical mass of orders, you ought to be able to put in your orders without sticking out as a price discoverer, because you are one of many.

On the flip side, there is also quantity discovery. That you surely want to be part of. As Peter Jenkins feeds his orders in to buy, Harold Bradley can be feeding in his orders to sell, and you are discovering quantity. I do not know why you would want to avoid a call market under those conditions.

JENKINS: From what Harold Bradley said before, it is easier to give the order up to an intermediary. With a pure call, there should be no need for an intermediary. You are making the decision; you are setting the price; you put it in. What happens is you give your orders over to a broker, because you are paying for a service then.

ROBERT SCHWARTZ [From the Floor]: Harold, you also suggested that you are doing it because a lot of traders on the buyside desks do not want to take the blame for a poor trade. The call market is like a train where you are just commuting with a lot of other people. You can leave your home whenever you want by car, and you can arrive at your office whenever the traffic allows. And if you make a wrong turn in maneuvering to beat the traffic, that is your fault. But if you are going in on a train with a couple hundred other people, then it is not your fault.

JENKINS: I have said this to Bill Lupien. I keep hearing that OptiMark is very difficult to use. I do not see how typing in "buy 5,000 shares at 20" is that difficult. The problem is that you are afraid of the outcome, that you might actually buy the stock –

BRADLEY: Exactly right. You cannot cancel up close.

KIM BANG: It seems that a call auction is a perfect solution, particularly for large imbalances, in the pre-open session. One of the difficulties is submitting an order in a marketplace where you may end up buying near the high of the day, or selling near the low. When you report that execution back to your portfolio manager, you know that you are not going to look great, particularly if your trade is compared to the VWAP.

BRADLEY: VWAP is the problem. Is that what you are saying?

WOOD: Well, VWAP and the crossing exhibit this aversion to price discovery.

Kim, as I understand it, at the open Bloomberg has to eat some trades. Its customers see other trades out there on SelectNet that they want, but cannot get, because they are gone by the time their orders get there. Would an opening call take some of the pressure off of SelectNet and help you?

BANG: Yes. The call market solution is an ideal concept for opening a market in an orderly fashion. The question is whether it should be a central marketplace, orchestrated by Nasdaq, or more of a virtual call action, where you have multiple participants who go in voluntarily. Bloomberg's Tradebook has created integrated electronic linkages into some of these crossing systems, particularly Investment Technology Group's POSIT, that allow a participant to be in a continuous environment while at the same time participating in the periodic crosses with minimum down time.

There is nothing negative about having a continuous session together with a call market. That is the direction the marketplace is taking us. We now have extended market hours.[89] Those extended hours will also help smooth out and dampen some huge imbalances, as investors start to participate more internationally, and as retail investors in particular become better educated.

BRADLEY: Let me ask a question. Benn, can you explain just how these European markets have handled the integration of calls to open their markets, which is something that Nasdaq cannot seem to achieve?

BENN STEIL: If you want to keep the current Nasdaq structure and jam it into a call, it is obviously impossible. The key point is simple: you have to get rid of the market orders at the time of the call. After the call is completed, you can easily satisfy all of the market orders with the market makers. It is only the limit orders that have to be fed into the call.

JENKINS: Even if you leave a market order in there, there is always a price.

STEIL: You may wind up with an order imbalance that clearly has to be cleaned up after the call. But in any normal call auction, you are going to wind up with unsatisfied orders left over at the end. The point is that limit

[89] Extended trading hours were actively promoted and introduced by market players at the height of the recent stock market boom. However, since then, after-hours trading in the US markets is not significant, indicating that investors still prefer trading during the regular sessions. Lack of liquidity, wider spreads, and costly operational factors are deterrents to successful after-hours sessions.

orders must be fed into the call to establish the clearing price. The market orders can then be satisfied on the basis of that clearing price. It is not terribly complicated. But if you are a market maker, and you do not want to give up that client order flow to a call, you will have problems supporting one.

BRADLEY: What you are saying then is that the New York Stock Exchange does not have a call either because of the inclusion of market orders?

JENKINS: That is correct. And the NYSE has battled that for years, especially at the close, in structuring around the limit orders.

GEORGE SOFIANOS: Let's talk about the difference between the opening call at the NYSE, and the problem you are having with the so-called closing call.

I believe call auctions work well if they are preceded by a period of non-trading. That is why the NYSE opening call works very well, because there is the overnight period of non-trading.

At the NYSE's closing call, orders accumulate and we see the imbalance. We try to attract liquidity by announcing this imbalance, by revealing how the imbalance builds up. We have found that the imbalance is valuable information. Suppose that a buying imbalance is announced at 3:50 p.m. What was the price before the closing call? People are trading on that very valuable information about the closing imbalance, and it seeps liquidity out of the closing call. It is hard to have a call auction with a continuous auction. Paris has a five-minute trading halt before the closing call, for that reason.

JENKINS: Doesn't New York technically have a five-minute period because most of the auctions actually go off 10 to 15 minutes after four o'clock?

SOFIANOS: What we want to encourage is competition among markets and between different business models. The Exchange is finally moving in that direction in terms of leveling the playing field. Rule 390 is gone, almost two weeks ago.[90] Now we are going to show the book and also provide direct access to the floor.[91]

We currently have different business models competing. The market, and brokers on the buyside, will decide on a level playing field, on where to

[90] NYSE Rule 390 prohibited NYSE members from trading stocks listed before April 1979 away from the floor.

[91] The repeal of Rule 390 meant that NYSE member firms could start making markets away from the floor in all listed stock, forcing the NYSE to provide more transparency and to become more competitive with dealers making markets in more of their listed securities.

direct their order flow. I used to be proud to say that we have a turnaround time of 22 seconds. If I say that now, people laugh at me.

But, that is a legitimate model. If there is a competing venue out there, and it is the right model, then we will lose business. That is how the floor is going to close down. You are not going to legislate the floor to close down. It is a business model decision of the New York Stock Exchange. And if you do not deliver the nice executions that Paul Davis mentioned earlier on, again you are going to go out of business.

WILLIAM LUPIEN, OptiMark [From the Floor]: If the order imbalance information is of so much value that we see the market move right before the close, isn't that also true pre-opening? Who gets to see that information? It is the specialist who sees it, and he could make a lot of money off of that opportunity every day. I used to make about thirty percent of my profits on the opening.

BANG: At least Nasdaq has some level of transparency in the marketplace, with its locked and crossed markets.

SOFIANOS: The specialist shares the information with the floor, and as part of this, shows the book. We are going to provide electronic ways of showing some of that information upstairs. As I have said, the extent to which the specialists improve their opening prices by participating or not is an empirical issue. In fact, there are some studies which show that the specialist does improve the opening price of the New York Stock Exchange.

WOOD: A specialist who is 100,000 shares short is not an innocent bystander.

WILLIAM CHRISTIE: At which points during the trading day should call markets be integrated into the Nasdaq market?

JUNIUS PEAKE, University of Northern Colorado [From the Floor]: I have a question first, if I may. I have argued for years that we really need is to have all orders as limit orders. The reason there is a market order is that you do not have sufficient information to price it. If you have sufficient information to price it, you can put a limit price on an order. The beauty of a limit order is that you never need a circuit breaker. If you have a bid and an offer that have a gap, you have a natural circuit breaker per stock.

A circuit breaker in electrical terms is used for two things: either an overload or a defective piece of equipment. If we have an overload in the stock market, we need to increase its capacity to handle order flow. If we have a defective stock market, I might even have an idea about how to fix it. Any comments?

PAUL DAVIS, Tiaa-Cref [From the Floor]: I will argue for market orders, on two levels. First, Harold Bradley and Peter Jenkins were saying that it is hard for the buyside trader to stand up and set a price. A market order is a good way to do that. Secondly, perhaps we should not use the language of market orders. We can use language from the English auctions, such as “a reserve price.” In an English auction, the auctioneer says, "What am I bid for this?" And the auctioneer starts low. In a way, that is like a market order. Starting in this way, with a low price, generates interest in the auction.

BRADLEY: I would disagree strenuously. My firm and I do not have a problem putting prices on orders. We do about 75 percent of our Nasdaq trading on ECNs which are nothing but limit orders. Our ten largest trades in the last quarter were around $70 million in a single day in a single stock on ECNs, all broken up with limit orders.

The problem I have with the marketplace is when large institutions have traders who are paid a lot of money call a broker and give him 100,000 shares and say, “go along with whoever is willing to pay up to the next highest level, but, by the way,” and this is a real term folks, “*participate*, but do not *initiate*.” I do not know what that means in the context of price discovery.

ROBERT SCHWARTZ, Baruch College [From the Floor]: All this talk about market orders vs. limit order shows that there is a basic misunderstanding about call markets. A market order is a very different creature in a continuous market than in a call market. In a continuous market, a market order is not an order from somebody saying, “I do not know how to price the thing.” A market order is a way to make the statement, “I want to trade now at the posted price, I want the immediacy, and I want the certainty of getting my order executed.” In a call, a market order is nothing other than a very aggressively priced limit order.

BRADLEY: That is correct. It is a buy order priced at infinity. It is a sell order priced at zero.

ROBERT SCHWARTZ [From the Floor]: I want to return to a previous question that was not answered. If Nasdaq puts in a call market, at what time of the day will they introduce it? One would certainly expect that it would be at the open.

CHRISTIE: Obviously, at the open. One current concern is with the capacity to handle all of the messages that arrive prior to the opening and shortly thereafter. There are a lot of messages because they are trying to figure out what the price is. If we had a mechanism like a call auction to figure out what the price is, a lot of those messages would disappear. That capacity issue can be solved, simply by having the auction.

Another obvious time to have a call is on the close, but I do not see a problem. These guys can probably determine, better than I can, if there is a problem in Nasdaq at the close. I do not see one. The evidence I have looked at says that, even though somewhat imperceptible, spreads tend to be narrowest right near the close.

SOFIANOS: How about using a call to launch an IPO?

CHRISTIE: That gets to our non-trading period issue. The best time to have them is after a period of non-trading.

SOFIANOS: You run into a problem with the membership of both the New York Stock Exchange and Nasdaq. The opening is probably the most profitable trading period in the entire day. These guys are not going to roll over easily. You basically need the SEC to come in and mandate a call market opening. It appears the SEC is not inclined to do this. At least at this point, the Commission prefers to see competitive market forces make these changes. I suggest that, among the alternative trading systems in the ECN community, we will come up with something creative. I am not sure what exactly the solution is, but I am pretty confident that we are moving in the right direction with connectivity.

BRADLEY: I want to respond to two things about the close that I think are prima facie evidence that a call is needed at that time of the trading day. One is the increasing preponderance of orders from the buyside that the sellside stops against the New York close or Nasdaq close. These are printed in London off the tape and then worked out a day later. To me this is evidence that we need a call, and that there is a problem.

The second bit of prima facie evidence is all of the orders that trade on Instinet's Crossing Network, and on other venues that are not reported to the tape, except under SEC regulation that allows firms to group those off-tape trades and report them only once a month. We market participants do not see volume done at that price. Wouldn't we be better off consolidating those orders at a time when everybody is sitting at the desk trying to get their orders executed?

WOOD: That is the motivation – do the trade in London and avoid the transparency of the print.

BRADLEY: There has been a fundamental change in the way block trades are created.

When you do a block trade, you are renting a broker's capital. The rent is increasingly costly as the broker's risk of distribution is increasingly out of line with the commission paid and prices accepted by institutional clients. If you are a mutual fund that pays a broker big-time commissions, you expect a broker to run a loss ratio. If you've got a problem with a stock, you get the dealer to bid for it and immediately transfer your risk. I have heard from brokers that they are petrified that hedge funds and competitors will bury them if those trades make it to the tape.

Sometimes, institutions may even shop the same block to several brokers. The publishing of that trade will put a broker at immediate risk in the marketplace. The block trading margins cannot justify this risk unless block trades are paid on the basis of charitable acts. In going to London, large traders are hiding from the tape. Our current market structures do not support that kind of block crossing utility.

OptiMark would get us in the right direction. AZX would get us there. But the rules allow too many people to get a free look at order books and then to use that information to 'trade ahead' of the auction. If a buyside trader puts a block up in London and is wrong, he or she can blame the broker. A trader utilizing a system like OptiMark, or the AZX, is 'on the hook' if he misreads the market. There is nobody to blame. A trader can't require OptiMark or AZX to use his capital to fix a trade that a buyside trader misses while trying to decide what to do. Brokers provide lots of free options to clients. Non-intermediated systems do not provide hedges for less than skillful traders.

WOOD: Has anyone made money putting in call markets that are not crosses but true call auctions?

STEIL: The only place, to the best of my knowledge, that it has been tried is in the US, and without success.

WOOD: How come?

STEIL: First, because of the focus on certain simplistic standards for performance measurement. In particular, VWAP is clearly inappropriate on the buyside trading desk. The incentive structure it promotes is not conducive to using systems like this. If you use a call auction, you do have to put a price on your order, and you are much more likely to fall afoul of VWAP standards. If you are playing for safety in terms of personal performance evaluations, you are not likely to use a call mechanism. You will prefer much more passive methods of trading, particularly those which minimize intraday market impact, even at the expense of poorer performance measured over the multiday life of the order.

Second, a trading desk should in principle be the agent of the portfolio manager, because the desk is implementing the portfolio manager's investment decisions. But from my discussions with portfolio managers and Chief Information Officers, they know little of the trading process, and care even less. Basically, the trading desk is accountable only to itself.

Finally, the whole business of soft dollar commissions, particularly with regard to listed stocks in the United States, provides a big disincentive, not only to using call auctions, but also to using electronic systems generally. People ask why ECNs have been so unsuccessful in the listed market (they are doing only about five percent of listed volume). This is not just a question of market structure, or of NYSE Rule 390. It is also because soft commissions in the United States applies overwhelmingly to listed securities (since Nasdaq trades have traditionally been done net), and over half of the institutional commissions in the US are targeted to specific brokers in advance.[92] Those targeted trades are not execution cost sensitive.

Consequently, the buyside has no incentive to use these systems to reduce their costs. And remember, soft commissions are a very good vehicle for fund management firms to pass on their operating costs to fund holders without the fund holders knowing the extent to which fund managers can soft their expenses. They do not have to pass on the cost to the investor in the form of a highly visible management fee.

JENKINS: You are saying that the trading desks are not accountable for their costs? Is that because the firms have no way to measure the costs? At our firm there is an understanding (or at least an idea) of how much it should cost us to get in or out of a position. We have studies which tell us our trading costs in percentage terms for each trader. With this measure we can gauge or estimate our cost of execution. If costs are, for example, 2% on average to get in or out of a position, and if these costs have been rising for any number of reasons, management takes notice. Management will also discuss the results with the portfolio team as well as with the trader. The traders are paid a base salary as well as a subjective bonus. One of the factors impacting the bonus level is trading performance.

WOOD: What do you use as a benchmark?

JENKINS: We use the Plexus "Alpha Capture" product. The benchmark used is called PAEG/L. PAEG/L is a proprietary benchmark created from the data that Plexus collects from their 80 or more institutional clients. Obviously, it is not a perfect system, but it provides our managers with an estimate of what costs are and of how they are trending. The traders are accountable for their actions.

STEIL: I have spent quite a bit of time on your trading desk, and there is no doubt in my mind, having seen other trading desks, that yours and Harold Bradley's are exceptionally well managed. But that is because you and Harold decided to make an issue of trading cost.

[92] Soft dollars apply in commission-based institutional trades. Until the introduction of decimal pricing, soft dollars were primarily associated with the listed markets where an agency system of trading predominates. However, since the introduction of decimal pricing on Nasdaq and rule changes by the SEC, some experts and trading professionals say that soft dollars will become a larger component of institutional trades on the Nasdaq market. The largest Nasdaq dealers are executing institutional trades for commissions, commission equivalents or on a risk less principal basis. Before the switch to decimal pricing, net, or spread-based trading in principal transactions was widespread on Nasdaq. The switchover, however, reportedly crimped profit margins for dealers because many OTC stocks started trading in increments of a penny. Now, 70% of institutional trades among the top 25 dealers on Nasdaq are handled for commissions, according to a Traders Magazine survey of market makers in 2002.

For years, Harold's firm, American Century, has been doing well over half of its Nasdaq orders electronically. If you are benchmarked in a different firm, that benchmark will be set on the basis of the vast bulk of your volume going through traditional, more expensive centers. You are not going to come up with the same challenging benchmark that, for example, Harold's firm will come up with.

One further point. Bob Schwartz mentioned the difference between market orders and limit orders, depending on which environment you are working in. In a study a few years ago, Donald Keim and Ananth Madhaven [93] looked at investor trading strategies and their relation to order placement. They found that, for so-called growth investors, 97 percent of their orders were market orders. Well, if you are going to trade like that, you are never going to use a call auction. And according to the study, what type of investors were most likely to use limit orders? Value investors, naturally, who are now extinct. The study found that nearly 77 percent of value investors' orders were market orders. So, if you are going to trade like that, you cannot participate in a call auction.

There are other parts of the world where call auctions have been more successful, but those have tended to be in emerging markets where they have started completely from scratch. The best example is the Warsaw Stock Exchange. When they rebuilt the market in 1991, they started only with call auctions on a weekly basis. They moved to daily calls in 1994. Then, as the stocks became more liquid, Warsaw did add (in 1996) continuous trading on top of the call auctions. Over half of their volume is still done through the calls. This is because investors in this market have learned to trust it. The price in a call market, particularly in a transition economy like Warsaw's, has a lot of integrity. You know that you are getting the same price as the Prime Minister's brother. That means something when you are building a market up from scratch.

BRADLEY: Over the last three years, since the introduction of the new order handling rules,[94] our ability to trade at increasingly lower and lower

[93] "Anatomy of the Trading Process: Empirical Evidence on the Motivation for and Execution of Institutional Equity Trades," Donald B. Keim and Ananth Madhavan, *Journal of Financial Economics* 37, 1995, pp. 371-398.

[94] On January 20, 1997, the National Association of Securities Dealers Automated Quotation (Nasdaq) system began a phased implementation of new Securities and Exchange Commission (SEC) order-handling rules designed to increase the access of individuals to the Nasdaq market and to reduce individuals' transactions costs. The order-handling rules were implemented for the fifty most active stocks on January 20, 1997, for the next fifty most active stocks on February 10, 1997, and for the next fifty most active stocks on February 24, 1997.

fractional prices on ECNs and Nasdaq stocks has been extraordinary. It has been absolutely unbelievable to us. We did $12 billion of business in the last six months at negative costs, as measured by our data provider.

Over the ten years that we have been gathering that data, the main line broker-dealers on Wall Street that have represented us have vacillated historically in about a 200 or 300 basis point range for round-trip all in trading costs. The range has not changed. Interestingly, our costs have risen over the last three years on listed securities. Right now, our costs for trading Nasdaq securities are below that of listed securities. That speaks to the issue of the protectionism that we have thrown up to the lack of ability at this point to trade listed stocks electronically. Why can't we get that?

WOOD: In other words, you cannot buy at the bid as easily?

BRADLEY: Never.

WOOD: You never can?

BRADLEY: That is a free option.

KAI-OLIVER MAURER, Deutsche Börse [From the Floor]: I have a European perspective, and may not know much about the details of the U S securities markets. But let me first ask, what would you do with the orders in a call auction within a form of continuous trading? Would you have two different audit books for these two trading forms? Second, what do you think would happen if you had a call auction at the same time as a continuous trading process? In Germany we do not have that.

BRADLEY: First, I think a call market will work. I do not believe the driver will be the buyside, unless we have significant regulatory change. It is just like the ECNs. About 80 percent of the business on ECNs is still conducted by broker/dealers on behalf of the buyside's agent.

The integration of a call into a continuous market can happen in one of two ways. Either with a time-out (as it is done in Germany), or, if it works effectively and establishes a clearing price, people will naturally find their way to it anyway without having to first have a time out. You are going into the auction at noon; am I going to send an order there? If somebody is worried about looking bad, are they going to put a trade up in the continuous market two minutes before the call auction? Everybody says that if you put an order into an auction that trades a dollar above or a dollar below where the last price was, you would look bad. Well, I guess I would look bad if I just sold it at a dollar lower right before the auction. Remember, there are two parties to every trade.

KAI-OLIVER MAURER [From the Floor]: Wouldn't you say that there is also a concern that continuous trading might stop around the time of the auction?

BRADLEY: Continuous trading would stop naturally as people deferred to the clearing mechanism of the call.

BANG: There is a somewhat mundane but real problem as well. The institutional buyside trader, particularly around those heavy volume periods in the morning, is working many different orders across several different markets with several different brokers, alternative trading systems, and ECNs. The alternative trading systems and ECNs tend to be more labor intensive. They require more action on a continuous basis.

Being able to participate in numerous venues of liquidity is a tricky proposition. It is up to the alternative trading systems and ECNs to have more linkages and better technology to enable participation in a continuous environment, as well as in a periodic call environment. All that without having an outage, so that the opportunity cost of working an order is minimized. We are getting there.

CHRISTIE: The other reason why we could have these periodic calls in our marketplace while simultaneously running a continuous market is that, in most cases, as somebody said before, you are only showing a small portion of your order to the marketplace. Most buyside traders keep the bulk of a large order hidden behind a smaller order. POSIT's success stems from the fact that people are just allocating a small portion of their orders to that venue.

BANG: Look into the future. There is an opportunity for us to develop smart, intelligent liquidity search engines, kind of like the Internet search engines, that locate liquidity and intelligently direct orders. It could be in a call auction. It could be in a cross. It could be locating an institution with a particularly large opposing position in a security while overlaying a negotiation feature to facilitate large block-size transactions.[95]

WOOD: The computer is really good at consolidating across various venues. I strongly favor the idea of competing market venues. You could concentrate all of your order flow in one spot. But, by definition, you would then have a monopoly, and monopolists resist technology and change.

You will get much better results in trading cost reduction with competing market venues, even if you fragment your order flow because of them. Competing venues are informationally linked and are not really fragmented. Computers are good at straddling various pools of liquidity. They can consolidate the pools on traders' desktops.

SOFIANOS: Kim Bang's point goes back to ITS and why the NYSE is proposing its elimination. Given technology, the market can do a much better job. The regulator has to require all markets to display the book, and

[95] Liquidnet is an anonymous trading system, founded by Seth Merrin, that directly brings together buyside firms, bypassing dealer intermediaries buying or selling blocks of stocks. As of mid-2002, Liquidnet had about 126 participants and daily volume of about six million shares.

to use open architecture that is searchable by the search engines. Then you will have a market that would actually look for the best price, and even walk out the book to get the best price. What ITS is doing now is just giving you the inside quote. But the technology is out there, and once you open the books, the search engine is going to…

BRADLEY: Why would the NYSE argue that now is a good time to do away with ITS? It just spent a year arguing with the Pacific Coast Exchange about implementing OptiMark as part of the ITS function. I do not understand this.

SOFIANOS: That is exactly why we want to get rid of ITS. You cannot get linkages unless you require that all markets show their books. They must all open their books to these search engines.

BRADLEY: You mean by price-time priority within the market and displayed orders?

SOFIANOS: Time priority across markets is going back to CLOB. We cannot have it both ways.

BRADLEY: No, I mean in the New York market, where time priority does not exist now.

JENKINS: We have the trade through rule.

WOOD: What about price discovery. Is it working? I have tick data back to June 1968. I error filter the data before I use it. There are not many errors in tick data, but they are huge when they occur. In March of 1999, the error filters stopped working. I could never get them to converge because we started to see such terrific jumps in quotes and trades, and the interaction between the trades and quotes. They just would not work, and I had to completely redesign my algorithms.

I have been on the trading desk quite a bit lately. I have seen these patterns where traders are punching through liquidity barriers provided by the book with such intensity that the naturals step aside. It is like what we saw with portfolio insurance trading before the 1987 Crash. Now, this pattern is occurring in individual stocks. What is going on? In part it may be because, as the tick size gets smaller, the amount available at the NBBO, and perhaps above that, decreases. I guess that is natural. If you think about the shape of the supply and demand curves, the closer we get to an equilibrium price with smaller tick sizes, the less quantity there is to trade. Yet, at the same time, as the tick size gets smaller and smaller, we see trading volumes soaring. So, it is not that liquidity has decreased. Liquidity is there in a different manner than it was before. But, is price discovery working? Would a call market help with this erratic price behavior that we are seeing?

BANG: There is clearly an issue of being able to transact large blocks with one execution. It happens less frequently, but, as we said, the increasing trading volume provides the liquidity. However, it does so in many smaller pieces. And as we move to decimalization, those pieces will get even smaller.

BRADLEY: I want to share a term I learned recently. It's called window shading and it happens when a dealer understands the general trading pattern of a particular firm. Let's suppose a buyside trader for XYZ firm calls a broker looking for a meaningful call on capital to facilitate a large block trade. The buyside trader may have one million shares to move and look for a bid from the dealer on the first 250,000 shares to get him started. That is when the window shade kicks in. The dealer proceeds to take the stock down hard. The Wall Street firm is now long, and it owns the stock in inventory. The dealer hits the bids in the Street to a clearing price level. He then steps in and cleans up the million share block by buying 750,000 shares at an otherwise oversubscribed price. What the seller can't see is the pace and type of inquiries from buyers who are likely lined up at a price just below where the bid comes in. The dealer may loose money on the principal bid but he expects to profit on the snap back of the window shade when the buyers miss the print and chase the stock back up from unrealistically low levels.

JUNIUS PEAKE [From the Floor]: As far as decimal pricing is concerned, it would seem to me that we have learned that when you reduce the cost of something you sell more of it. And look what happened to volume when fixed commissions disappeared. It exploded.

BRADLEY: Fixed commissions have not gone away.

JUNIUS PEAKE [From the Floor]: In the fund business?

BRADLEY: No. Right now, commissions are higher than they were in 1975, adjusted for volume.

JUNIUS PEAKE [From the Floor]: Okay. But volume did go up. If you move to smaller trading increments, it will go up again for the same reason. Yes, there are structural defects that you pointed out, Harold, but the cost of trading is still down. The cost of trading is down on average from what it was. I remember when 50 cents a share was not uncommon. When somebody did 5,000 shares each day they were on target for the month and could go home.

SOFIANOS: The initiative among ECNs right now is direct connections. The next initiative is to share limit order books. Once you move to a decimalized marketplace, you are going to see many of the larger ECNs sharing large limit order books.[96] Some will agree to share limit orders

[96] The trend is towards more sharing of limit order books and easier access to the combined pool of ECN liquidity. In a manifestation of this, two individual ECNs would "pair off", sharing their books. The introduction of Nasdaq's SuperMontage, a major challenge for ECNs, could accelerate the trend. On another front, technology suppliers are stepping forward to build bridges. For example, SunGard Trading Systems, in March 2002,

books throughout the entire day, which means that you will have much greater breadth and depth of liquidity and the electronic access to that liquidity is going to be a very good thing. Some ECNs even give up the ability to internalize order flow in return for really providing best execution. Bloomberg Tradebook considers itself a leader in this category.

JENKINS: I do not understand this. If there is better linkage in the marketplace, and protection of limit orders, you have a deeper book. Now you go to decimals, and are trading in pennies. Why wouldn't retail investors want to be linked to the call market?

STEIL: This is the case in Europe. On-line retail investing exists in Europe, we just do not hear much about it. If you are in Milan or Paris, for example, and you are a retail investor, you can trade on the stock exchanges' books through a broker member of the exchange. Right now, all on-line trading in the US is basically e-mailing your order to a broker. Who knows what happens to the order after that? It depends on whether that particular brokerage firm happens to own an ECN or is a market maker. In other words, the order is routed to where it is in the best interests of that broker. Real on-line trading does exist in Europe because there you have proper, non-intermediated, on-line electronic trading systems.

WOOD: Doug Atkin said it was going to come soon through Instinet.

ROBERT SCHWARTZ [From the Floor]: Lets go back to the statement about the costs of trading having come down. Whether they have or not depends on how you measure costs. The easiest thing to capture in a measurement is something that you can directly see, like the spread or commissions.

But what can you say about trading costs in an environment where intra-day volatility is very high? Think again about the slide I showed this morning, the intra-day transaction record for Pfizer (see page xvi). Those price swings are not simply the result of news. They are not simply due to liquidity trading. It is because institutions are breaking up their orders. They are sending them to the market in small pieces. You have a lot of momentum. Price goes up. It can go up a dollar or more for a $50 stock. It can go up too high and then come back down. The swings are tremendous. They are reflective of high trading costs.

---

introduced an order delivery system called Powernet. The idea then was to enable dealers to connect with five ECNs BRUT, Archipelago, Redibook as well as Instinet and Island. Powernet was designed to integrate the central limit order books of these ECNs into one central system. Another vendor, Lava Trading, provides routing services to various ECNs. Meanwhile, Instinet and Island, once separate ECNs which on Sept. 20, 2002, completed their previously announced merger, now have a powerful incentive to share liquidity.

WOOD: Breaking up a large order into small pieces does not necessarily mean that you have more volatility.

ROBERT SCHWARTZ [From the Floor]: I linked it in with momentum. You break up your order. You feed it into the market over time. The market sees part of the order coming in. They know that more is coming.

JENKINS: I would disagree with that. When you are in an ECN, you are trading in smaller lots, and yet there is information on even the smallest lots traded. The larger the number of trades in smaller lots, the more information that is put out, and it moves the market because of certain players in the market. I do think that this increases volatility.

ROBERT SCHWARTZ [From the Floor]: Yes, agreed. But I was not thinking of ECNs, per se. The accentuated volatility is a market wide phenomenon. Price, for instance, will not just trend up – it will trend up too far. Then it reverses and goes back down. These accentuated, reversing moves translate into volatility.

BRADLEY: There is another volatility-related point. If Peter Jenkins puts up 50,000 shares at a price with a broker, and I have got five of these resting market orders or "participate" orders. Think of what happens to the process. We have created a process like internalization of retail order flow. The big institutional brokerage business is nothing but a huge internalization business. The dealers, in this case, basically stop their customers' orders against big trades. As a result, when a big trade happens, you all of a sudden have disadvantageously committed your capital to protect a customer.

It is like what the regional exchanges do with what is called primary market protection. Say I try to send an order to the Pacific Coast Exchange. The Pacific Coast Exchange then sends it immediately to the New York Stock Exchange because it cannot reconcile a price order that interferes with its economic model that allows brokers to internalize retails orders. That is the whole market structure issue, that is what creates volatility -- nobody is pricing orders.

But a call market gets us there. The real issue is that most traders use market orders or some sort of "stop" or "participate" strategy and nobody is using limit orders. So as soon as one person does not consummate a trade, the whole line of dominos that has been created falls down.

ROBERT SCHWARTZ [From the Floor]: So, let me ask all of you directly: is intra-day volatility inflated? Is it high?

BRADLEY: Is the market high? This is a Greenspan question. We will have to invoke Greenspan again.

ROBERT SCHWARTZ [From the Floor]: What do you think about intra-day volatility?

SOFIANOS: It is high, but market structure is not the reason.

ALLAN GRODY, Financial InterGroup Holdings [From the Floor]: You are all trying to hide orders from each other. Why aren't you willing to show size anonymously, within the crossing networks or within the existing call markets? How come volume has not taken off there? That is what would seem to be the natural place for you to go to get liquidity.

JENKINS: I agree, knowledge leaks out. I cite OptiMark. Bill Lupien comes in to speak to us. I am in shock. For large order flow, I cannot understand, there is – as far as I'm concerned – there is no way that that order can be leaked. I do not understand it. Even if you have a large order, you run it through a system like that, it takes seconds, it comes back, and now you are in the regular market and knowledge leaks out.

BRADLEY: It goes farther than that. Many buyside firms have insufficient order management system technology. The buyside has not made the costly systems investment as have profit-seeking block trading firms. This is basic Economics 101. The buyside pays for brokerage services with client commissions. Those commissions come out of performance and receive little investor scrutiny. There is virtually no accountability. If there is a little slippage on a trade, the trader screams and yells and tells his portfolio manager how bad the Street is. The alternative is major systems upgrades and, in some cases, talent upgrades. Those costs are hard dollar costs. They don't come out of client pockets but out of money manager pockets. Those costs reduce a money manager's profits, and possibly the trader's bonus. There is little incentive for buyside firms to make that kind of investment absent better guidance on best execution obligations and record keeping.

SOFIANOS: I disagree. Not every desk has 50 mega size orders sitting in front of them every day. At most trading desks, there are three large orders sitting in front of them.

BRADLEY: So they should be able to do it.

SOFIANOS: To type those orders in a system is not difficult.

HOLLY STARK, Kern Capital Management [From the Floor]: Most of the buyside gets their information from the sellside.

UNIDENTIFIED SPEAKER: George, the probability of having two opposing large orders is also somewhat

MIKE DRITZ, Dritz Enterprises [From the Floor]: This relates to change too, and I think they have resisted change. Historically, change has meant things that have not been good for the brokerage industry. There is a lot of technology out there, probably more than we would know what to do with. The problem is that there are many people who are not too comfortable with technology. There are a lot of people on both sides of the Street who say that they know how to use technology, but lock them in a room, give them a computer, and ask them to plug it in. They cannot do it.

OptiMark is a wonderful system and it should work, but people do not know how to plug it in. They should take the time, make the effort, and learn how to use a new system.

PAUL DAVIS [From the Floor]: Kim, you were speaking about the connectivity between the different ECNs. Are there any regulatory hurdles that would stand in the way of ECNs getting together and instituting a call auction?

BANG: Certainly not in the over-the-counter market. There is nothing to prevent ECNs from getting together and introducing a call on OTC issues. But there are regulatory barriers to competition on the listed markets, such as the rules of the ITS. These would prevent the ECNs from running a call auction away from the New York Stock Exchange. All of this is more of an evolutionary and regulatory issue than a technology issue.

The various business models are not perfectly aligned. Some ECNs, for instance, are happy to share their limit order books throughout the entire trading session. Some are willing to do it only for the pre and post primary market hours. Some ECNs are closed systems. Data dissemination and access may be available only to subscribers. They only allow participant-to-participant participation. There are two or three ECNs that are working towards greater transparency and access. I think that we will move in the direction of more transparent, virtual access among multiple liquidity providers.

BRADLEY: Mike Dritz, I think you are partially right, but it is more about how we do business traditionally, than about resistance to change. I will get a young person on our desk to handle the small electronic orders. He picks it up within two days.

WOOD: This has been great fun. I would like to give each of the panel members a chance to summarize his thoughts.

BANG: I would say that if we are looking for an immediate, single-price open solution, it has to come from the SEC. Over time, we could get there through the alternative trading systems and ECNs. I believe it was said that we are going to see competition evolve in a multi-dimensional manner among exchanges, ECNs, ATSs, and SROs, as well as among brokers and dealers and desktop application liquidity portals. This competition is going to lead to a more efficient National Market System. It will be more innovative than the current model and it will provide greater choice for investors. Investors will benefit with the access to more liquidity and a more vibrant capital markets system where innovation and competition are essential.

Over time, the marketplace will evolve towards a better model with the advances in ATSs in the pre and post primary sessions, as well as through the inevitable participation of more users of these systems.

Technology and competition are a good thing for a marketplace. It is good for investors, and over time it will be an increasingly better marketplace. As Harold Bradley mentioned, his execution costs for over-the-counter Nasdaq securities are actually below those of the New York Stock Exchange. Historically, this has certainly not been the case. It is a clear testimony to the success of the SEC order-handling rules, and the creation of ECNs which are competing in the National Market System. As long as we continue on this road, we will have a better National Market System for investors.

BRADLEY: Anonymity. Price-time priority within markets. Decimals. Disintermediated electronic access. That means totally un-intermediated electronic access, to all markets, including those in New York. Pure electronic calls to open and to close the market, and a block trading facility like OptiMark, with global linkages. Then I will get off the lecture circuit.

WOOD: We would miss you Harold. But we won't hold our breath.

JENKINS: The technological competition is out there to produce a call auction for the Nasdaq and the New York Stock Exchange. We have many entrepreneurs coming into our offices offering solutions to trading demands. I have heard buyside traders express their concerns with both the Nasdaq and New York opening for quite some time. Both markets could benefit from a call auction. It's more efficient and could provide greater liquidity if the trading community sees that it is fair and orderly. Traders tend to shy away from entering large orders into the New York open because they feel they could be gamed. A call auction could increase participation from the institutional community. So, if Nasdaq is going to say that over the last six years they have not been able to figure out a way to put in a call structure for the opening, I am comfortable that some of the technology companies out there, or some other independent providers, are going to offer that solution.

SOFIANOS: Harold, going down your list of anonymity, price-time priority, decimals, and direct access, compared to five years ago you have to admit that we are more or less halfway there. So if you do not give up, and if you continue hammering at us, you may get us all the way there in the next five years.

I was a bit alarmed by the direction of the discussion towards the end here. There is this notion that there are all of these wonderful systems that have not been able to attract order flow, and that this is the fault of the users not recognizing how good these systems are (with the exception of Peter Jenkins and Harold Bradley). It is a dangerous argument, and it is a discouraging argument. It stifles the urge to innovate. That is not the answer.

There are some fundamental problems. In particular, how to balance the need for some transparency but not total transparency. OptiMark is a great system, but it may have moved too far in the direction of having no transparency whatsoever. That is the heart of the issue.

Market fragmentation is not an issue over the fragmentation of the displayed orders. The fragmentation issue is a huge pool of liquidity that is not displayed. It is either reserve orders, or it is orders held on the floor of the exchange. We have not yet found an electronic system that will encourage the displaying of the liquidity to balance this trade-off. It is not because the users are stupid and do not get it.

CHRISTIE: Once Nasdaq figures out how to conduct a call auction, they may elect to do one at the open. Another place to use them would be after a trading halt to reopen the market. Nasdaq does not advertise that they have trading halts. They advertise that they are open for business from 9:30 to 4:00, but they are not. They have trading halts on news pending. The average length is about an hour. The market makers have a whopping five minutes to start quoting that stock before they begin trading it again.

The work that I have done with Jeff Harris and Shane Corwin[97] says that those spreads on New York stocks go from maybe 25 cents to 30 cents. At the reopen on Nasdaq, they go from about 25 cents to 85 cents. It does not last long, but for those first couple of minutes, price discovery is absolutely horrible after a trading halt. That seems to be a natural place for this call auction to work.

STEIL: George has slightly mischaracterized the problem or the lack of success so far of call auctions. I do not think it is just that users have not "appreciated" the virtues of these systems. First of all, the incentive structure under which the buyside is currently operating does not give them much motivation to use these systems. Also, consider the nature of the relationship between the buyside and the sellside. They do not have much confidence in the ability of the SEC to address this issue. In 1996, the SEC did a big sweep of broker-dealer firms and found that two-thirds of soft commission agreements were unwritten.[98] They are unwritten for a reason,

[97] "The Impact of Market Mechanisms on Prices, Trading Activity, and Execution Costs," William Christie, Shane Corwin, and Jeff Harris, *Journal of Finance 57 (3)*, 2002, pp. 1443-1478.

[98] An SEC probe into soft dollar practices was launched in the fall of 1996. The 22-month review resulted in the Inspection Report on the Soft Dollar Practices of Broker-Dealers, Investment Advisers and Mutual Funds, released on September 22, 1998. The Report highlighted shortcomings in the industry with respect to the use of soft dollars and called for more and better disclosure, stricter record-keeping requirements, and the implementation of internal compliance procedures by investment advisers and broker-dealers. See also, "Controlling Institutional Trading Costs: We Have Met the Enemy, and They are Us," Robert Schwartz and Benn Steil, *The Journal of Portfolio Management*, Spring 2002.

and that is very, very difficult to regulate away. The big firms did not want the regulators examining their questionable soft-dollar arrangements too closely.

So, is there a market solution to all of this? There probably is. Given that the execution cost advantage for these systems is increasing, those that are able to take the biggest advantage of them will, in the end, most likely be the most profitable. Who are those firms? In my view, the fund managers who will be the most profitable in the future will be in the integrated sellside/buyside houses. In other words, we are talking about very large financial institutions like Morgan Stanley, Goldman Sachs, and Merrill Lynch.

Why do I say this? These firms already have the analysts. They already have the research capabilities. They already have the trading systems. In other words, they do not have to pay for them through soft commissions. They can cover the cost of these services internally across the entirety of their operations, not just in trading. For example, they can cover the costs via their primary market business, their investment advisory business, and all sorts of things like that. It will be those firms that are best able to take full advantage of the benefits of electronic trading in general, and of call auctions in particular.

WOOD: The single greatest reduction in trading cost that I can visualize comes from the buyers and sellers naturally providing liquidity to one another. This happens so nicely in a call auction. We will achieve the greatest reduction in trading cost by getting rid of the barriers that keep natural buyers and sellers from supplying liquidity to one another. We will always need intermediaries, because there will always be imbalances. But with networks and computers, it is easier to find the other side, and when it is easier to find the other side, intermediaries ought to be downsized. And/or, they must learn to be faster on their feet.

Afterword

Three electronic, price discovery call auctions have been used in the United States, and each received major attention at the conference: AZX's Arizona Stock Exchange, OptiMark, and State Street's Bond Connect. The attendees viewed each auction as an experiment. All of them are now inactive. What conclusions should be drawn? Why did the experiments fail?

To answer these questions, let us first recognize that call auctions fit into three categories, in ascending levels of complexity:

On the simplest level are the non-price discovery crossing networks such as Instinet's Crossing Network and ITG's POSIT.

On the next level, are auctions, such as the Arizona Stock Exchange, that cumulate participant limit orders (in descending order of price for buy orders, and in ascending order of price for sell orders) to find the value that maximizes the number of shares that trade.

On the most complex level, are auctions that allow participants to place a variety of conditions on their orders. These conditions might include the limit price on an order may depend on the number of shares available for purchase or sale, on the price of other securities, and/or on the value of a market index. OptiMark and Bond Connect fit into this third category.

There are several lessons we might learn from the experiments. The first is the importance of keeping a trading system simple. The crossing networks are simple, and they have succeeded handsomely. However, the Arizona Stock Exchange, because it includes price discovery, has faced a far more difficult challenge. OptiMark and Bond Connect, with their complex limit order capabilities, had a level of sophistication that market participants may not be willing to accept right now. Of course, no system, no matter what it can do, will succeed unless it draws sufficient order flow. Order flow is to a market, as gas is to an automobile – without it, a market will not go.

The second lesson we might learn from the experiments is how difficult it is for a new system to achieve critical mass order flow. The Arizona Stock Exchange, in particular, as a stand-alone system, suffered from this problem. But OptiMark and Bond Connect also faced this difficult challenge, even though they both were connected with established markets: OptiMark with the Pacific Stock Exchange and Nasdaq, and Bond Connect with the Boston Stock Exchange. If they had achieved critical mass order flow and sustained that volume, all three systems would undoubtedly have had far better performance characteristics then the experiments revealed. Each of the three facilities was designed for institutional customers. For all intents and purposes, each was marketed exclusively to institutional customers.

The third lesson from the experiments is how difficult it is to get institutional traders to place their orders in a system that has price discovery capability when retail customers are not present. Institutional traders like to hide in a crowd. They do not participate when they think that their own orders will affect price discovery. Unfortunately, when they alone comprise the market, a crowd is not likely to form. A price discovery call auction must also include retail customers. Neither the Arizona Stock Exchange nor Bond Connect did so.[99]

There is another lesson that we might learn from the OptiMark and Bond Connect experiments: a totally opaque price discovery call does not work well for institutional customers. Transparency is a critical characteristic of a trading system. Institutional investors want to know what is available on the other side of the market so that they might better gauge the market impact their orders are likely to have. But transparency may also lead to market impact, as knowledge of the existence of a large order commonly results in front running. The Arizona Stock Exchange offered transparency and a choice: customers could submit their orders to an open book (price discovery was based only on orders sent to the open book), or to a closed book that was effectively a crossing network (orders placed on this book would have no market impact). OptiMark and Bond Connect, on the other hand, were entirely black box systems used to protect against front running. Further, it is virtually impossible for calls in the third category of complexity to provide an open book because limit orders with multiple conditions placed on them cannot be simply arrayed and aggregated by price.

There is a final lesson to be learned. A call auction needs to achieve

[99] Retail orders did get entered into OptiMark because, at each call, the system swept the limit order books of the Pacific Stock Exchange.

critical mass each and every time it is run. This cannot be taken for granted, even for a facility that is well established. The reason is that each call starts with an empty book, and many participants (most importantly the large traders) do not wish to be the first to place their orders because of their reluctance to participate actively in price discovery. This underscores the importance of attracting retail customers to a call. Further, market makers should be imbedded in the auctions as animators to "seed" the book building process.[100]

Success for any new trading facility is difficult to achieve. Call auctions are no exception. In light of the five lessons discussed above, it is not surprising that the three experiments failed. Designing and instituting a well functioning call is, indeed, a challenge. There are many design alternatives, and "getting it right" is not easy. If a call is poorly designed, ineffectively implemented, and does not work, some observers will conclude that calls, categorically, are undesirable. This is unfortunate. A number of conference attendees (myself included) believe that well functioning, electronic call auctions would add appreciably to the efficiency of US equity markets. Hopefully, time will bear out the accuracy of our prediction.

Robert A. Schwartz

[100] The Arizona Stock Exchange did include this design feature.

Participant Biographies

Douglas Atkin was President and Chief Executive Officer of Instinet from 1998 until April 2002. From 1992 to 1998, Mr. Atkin served in London as Chief Executive Officer of Instinet International Limited, in charge of Instinet's non-US operations. Mr. Atkin joined Instinet in 1984.

Kim Bang joined Bloomberg Tradebook LLC as a founding member in April 1996. He assumed the title of President in December 1999. During this tenure, Bloomberg Tradebook has established itself as a leading electronic consolidator of global liquidity. Since its inception, US daily shares traded has risen to over 150 million and the daily value of international shares traded has risen to over $1 billion. Bloomberg Tradebook now offers its global customer base trading on 65 exchanges. Many leading buy-side institutions and broker-dealers have come to benefit from Bloomberg Tradebook's commitment to customer service and unique blend of innovative tools and trading algorithms that help them achieve better executions.

Mr. Bang has recently been appointed to Nasdaq's Quality of Markets Committee. Prior to joining Bloomberg Tradebook, Mr. Bang was President of Futech Capital Management, a hedge fund managing quantitative derivative strategies for institutional clients. Before joining Futech in 1993, he developed a European foreign exchange cross trading business for American International Group Trading Corp. From 1988-90, he created and developed a fixed income derivatives trading desk for Commerzbank in Luxembourg. His prior sales trading experience includes positions at BankAmerica Futures and Drexel Burnham Lambert.

Harold S. Bradley, Senior Vice President, leads the strategic ventures group for American Century, and is a member of the company's Strategic Planning Group and the Investment Oversight Committee.

Mr. Bradley joined American Century in 1988 and has acted in a variety of capacities in the investment management area of the firm. For two years, he was a mutual fund portfolio manager on the team that manages the Heritage Fund and the VP Capital Appreciation Fund. For ten years, Mr. Bradley directed the fund company's equity trading group. He has actively supported customer-oriented market reforms including limit order display rules, decimal quoting and trading of equity securities, and complete disclosure of investment adviser "soft dollar" practices.

Mr. Bradley serves on the boards of W.R. Hambrecht and Co. and StarMine Corporation. He also serves in an advisory capacity on the board of Archipelago Holdings, LLC. Prior to joining American Century, Mr. Bradley was a member of the Kansas City Board of Trade, where he traded stock index, financial and agricultural futures and options. He also served as marketing director for the exchange.

Mr. Bradley is a Summa Cum Laude graduate of Marquette University. He serves on the Investment Company Institute Task Force on Market Structure. He formerly served on the Institutional Traders Advisory Committee of the New York Stock Exchange, the NASDAQ Quality of Markets Committee and on the executive committee overseeing development of the Financial Information Exchange (FIX) protocol.

William J. Brodsky was named chairman and chief executive officer of the Chicago Board Options Exchange (CBOE) in December 1996. Under his direction, CBOE implemented many changes that have fortified CBOE's current position as the largest options marketplace in the world. CBOE experienced its best year ever in Fiscal Year 1999 – with total option volume, stock option volume, average daily volume and open interest all skyrocketing to record-breaking levels.

Initiatives launched by his administration include the formation of a Strategic Planning Task Force that conducted a comprehensive examination of the options business, resulting in a massive internal reorganization of staff and the floor wide expansion of CBOE's proprietary DPM (Designated Primary Market Maker) system to enhance customer service on CBOE's trading floor. In addition, CBOE began development of a screen-based trading system, CBOE*direct*™, while simultaneously upgrading CBOE's highly automated trading floor.

Mr. Brodsky began his career as an attorney in the securities industry with the firm of Model, Roland and Company in 1968. In 1974, Mr. Brodsky joined the American Stock Exchange (AMEX) where he became head of options trading in 1976 and served as executive vice president for operations between 1979 and 1982. He also served as the AMEX representative on the board of The Options Clearing Corporation. In 1994, the AMEX honored Mr. Brodsky for his role in the development of its options programs.

Mr. Brodsky joined the Chicago Mercantile Exchange (CME) in 1982 as executive vice president and chief operating officer. He was named president and chief executive officer in 1985, and served in that capacity until joining CBOE in February 1997. Perhaps the most enduring legacy of his 11-year term as president of the CME was in his role in product development, particularly in the area of stock index futures and options. Several of the instruments he developed were created in conjunction with the CBOE, including equity derivatives based on the Standard & Poor's® Indices, Nasdaq 100 Index®, Mexican IPC, S&P 500®/BARRA Growth and Value Indices and the Russell 2000® Index.

Mr. Brodsky serves as a director of the Peoples Energy Corporation, the Futures Industry Association and the Swiss Futures and Options Association. He is a member of the Federal Reserve Bank of New York's International Advisory Committee. Mr. Brodsky was selected for induction into the Derivatives Hall of Fame in April 2000. He also serves on the J.L. Kellogg Graduate School of Management Advisory Council, and as a trustee of Syracuse University. He is a member of the board of trustees of the Northwestern Memorial Hospital Corporation, where he chairs its Investment Committee and a member of the Council on Foreign Relations in New York City.

Mr. Brodsky holds an A.B. degree and a J.D. degree from Syracuse University and the Syracuse University School of Law and is a member of the bar in Illinois and New York.

William G. Christie, a native of Canada, received his undergraduate degree in Commerce from Queen's University, in Kingston, Ontario in 1978. He earned his MBA from the University of Chicago in 1980, and worked as a financial analyst at the Canadian operations of Hewlett-Packard and the Ford Motor Company before returning to Chicago to pursue his Ph.D. He completed his doctoral studies in 1989, and has taught at the Owen Graduate School of Management since leaving the University of Chicago.

Bill's research has been published in a wide range of academic journals, including the *Journal of Financial Economics*, the *Journal of Finance*, and the *Journal of Business*. He is co-author of the paper "Why do Nasdaq market makers avoid odd-eighth quotes?", which was awarded First Prize in the 1995 Smith Breeden Prize competition for outstanding papers published in the *Journal of Finance*. He has also received the Irwin Distinguished Paper Award from the Southwestern Finance Association for his research with fellow Owen colleague Roger Huang. He serves as an Associate Editor of the *Review of*

Financial Studies, and as co-editor of the *Journal of Financial Intermediation.* He also is a member of the Economic Advisory Board at the National Association of Securities Dealers. He has appeared on Marketplace Radio, CNBC's Inside Opinion and Market Wrap, the Wall Street Journal Report and CNN's Inside Business in conjunction with the Justice Department and SEC investigations of the Nasdaq market.

Bill was awarded the James A. Webb, Jr. Award for Excellence in Teaching in the regular MBA program in 1994, 1995, and 1998, and the Executive M.B.A. Program Outstanding Professor Award in 1993, 1994, and 1998. He was also awarded a Vanderbilt Chair of Teaching Excellence for the 1996-99 term. The purpose of the chair is to "recognize extraordinary accomplishment among Vanderbilt's teachers and to promote the further enhancement of teaching at Vanderbilt." In addition, he was promoted to Associate Professor of Management with tenure, effective September 1996. He was appointed the Associate Dean for Faculty Development at the Owen School in September 1999, and Dean of the Owen School in July 2000. He also holds the Ralph Owen Professorship in Finance, and is married to Kelly Christie, Director of Academic Programs and Student Services at Owen.

Paul Davis joined TIAA-CREF in 1983 after several years at Prudential-Bache Securities. Before that, he taught mathematics at Lehigh University and Manhattanville College. He is a graduate of West Virginia University and has a PhD in mathematics from Carnegie-Mellon University.

J.D. Delafield is the CEO of Delafield Hambrecht, Inc., an investment bank located in Seattle, WA. Prior to founding Delafield Hambrecht, he was a co-founder of WR Hambrecht + Co., a San Francisco investment bank. Previously, he worked at Morgan Stanley in New York and Singapore and for The Coca-Cola Company in Beijing. J.D. holds an AB from Princeton University and an MBA from Harvard Business School. J.D. and his wife Cecile have three children, Cate, Jack and Caroline.

Marianne Demarchi is Director of Strategic Marketing at the Marketing Division of Euronext, the first pan-European exchange born from the merger of the exchanges of Amsterdam, Brussels, Paris and Lisbon as well as London's International Financial Futures and Options Exchange (LIFFE).

Ms. Demarchi, who holds an MA and a PhD in Finance from the University of Aix-Marseille III, started her career in 1994 at the Research and Strategy Department of Société des Bourses Françaises. In 1999, she became Head of the Equity Research Department, and in September 2000 was appointed Manager of the R&D Cash Products Department.

As Euronext's Director of Strategic Marketing, she is in charge of the development and marketing of structured cash products, including exchange-traded funds (ETFs), warrants, certificates and bonds. She is also responsible for research into worldwide development of products and markets and for the production of data and statistics.

One of Marianne Demarchi's most recent achievements is the creation and launch of Next Track, the Euronext product segment specializing in ETFs. Before that, she was involved in developing the DJ STOXX indexes as a member of the Index Design Committee.

Ian Domowitz is Managing Director, ITG Products. Prior to joining ITG, Dr. Domowitz was the Mary Jean and Frank P. Smeal Chaired Professor of Finance at the Pennsylvania State University. He previously taught in the Economics Department and in the Kellogg Graduate School of Management, Northwestern University, and was a research associate, Center for the Study of Futures Markets, at Columbia University. He is the author of numerous research articles in the areas of finance, econometrics, statistics, and industrial organization, including work on the design, organization, and regulation of electronic trading market structures. He has served as a consultant to government and international organizations, including the Federal Reserve System, the Commodity Futures Trading Commission, the International Monetary Fund, and the World Bank, as well as to various securities exchanges and trading organizations. A former member of the NASD's Bond Market Transparency Committee, he also is the immediate past chair of the Economic Advisory Board of NASD. Dr. Domowitz received his Ph.D. in economics from the University of California.

Michael A. Dritz is Chair of Dritz Enterprises, LLC, a New York based investment firm, which also provides consulting services for the financial industry. In 1998, Michael Dritz was elected Chair of the Board for International Keystone Entertainment, an integrated entertainment company that produces theater-quality motion pictures for distribution in North America and internationally. He was previously a Managing Director for Merrill Lynch & Co. and Chair of its Smith Brothers International Advisory Division. He served as President and CEO of Smith New Court, Inc. and an Executive Director of Smith New Court PLC from 1985 until their acquisition by Merrill Lynch in 1995. He is former President of Dritz Goldring, Inc., a specialist firm on the NYSE and ASE and a past governor of the American Stock Exchange and Director of the Securities Industry Automation Corporation (SIAC).

William Freund served as the New York Stock Exchange's Senior Vice President and Chief Economist for 18 years (1968-1986). He was the New York Stock Exchange Professor of Economics at Pace University's Lubin School of Business from 1986 to 2001. He was Chairman of the Pace University's Graduate Department of Economics and International Business from 1986-1993. Since 1993, he has been, and remains, Director of the Pace

University Center for the Study of Equity Markets (now renamed the William C. Freund Center for the Study of Securities Markets).

From 1952 to 1962, he was Economist for the Prudential Insurance Company of America. From 1962 to 1965, he was Associate Professor of Finance and NYU's Graduate School of Business. He returned to Prudential as Chief Economist and Director of Investment Research between 1965 and 1968. His Ph.D. degree is from Columbia University. For twenty years, he was an economic adviser (pro bono) to four governors of New Jersey.

He has served on a number of corporate boards of directors, including Ecogen and, most recently, US Life Corp where he was actively involved in merging that company with the American General Insurance Company. He is author of several books including Investment Fundamentals, and co-author of People and Productivity. He has written chapters for numerous other books and has authored a large number of articles.

Allan Grody has been involved in the financial services industry for over 35 years. He was an early innovator in technology within the banking, securities and investment industries, continued to serve the financial industry as a consulting partner of a Big 8 firm, Coopers & Lybrand, where he founded their Financial Services Consulting Practice, and now is a private consultant and educator. Professor Grody founded and teaches a unique risk management systems course at NYU's graduate school of business, and guest lectures on financial market structures and financial information systems. He was an early innovator in securities and futures systems, financial industry communications systems, electronic trading, and retail and institutional automation. Throughout his career he has represented stock, options and futures exchanges as an expert witness. As an entrepreneur he developed an early version of personal financial planning software and the first functioning financial industry web site. He has authored numerous studies of the future application of information technology in the financial services industry. He holds a BS degree in mathematics from the City University of New York.

William Harts is Executive Vice President, Corporate Strategy for Nasdaq. His responsibilities include the initiation and development of strategic opportunities for the world's largest stock market. Until recently he was Managing Director of Strategic Business Development for the Global Equity Division of Salomon Smith Barney with responsibility for the firm's partnerships, joint ventures and investments as well as market structure developments relating to equity trading. Before taking on that role, Mr. Harts was co-head of the firm's Global Portfolio Trading operation, with responsibility for desks in New York, London and Tokyo. He began at SSB in September 1993 after working at Lehman Brothers where he established an automated market making and trading operation for the Worldwide

Equities Division. Prior to that, he worked at Goldman, Sachs & Co. in their Quantitative Strategies Group designing equity derivative risk analysis software and convertible bond trading systems. He is well known in the finance industry as an authority on financial markets, trading and applied technology and has been a featured speaker on market structure issues at many industry forums.

Mr. Harts has spoken before the Securities Industry Association Market Structure Conference, the Pace University Center for the Study of Equity Markets' Securities Industry Conference, and a panelist at the Baruch College Zicklin School of Business' Regulation of US Equity Markets Conference. Recently he was a member of the SEC Advisory Committee on Market Information.

Mr. Harts served as a Director and Vice Chairman and member of the Board of the Philadelphia Stock Exchange from 1994 through 1999. He has been a member of the Board of Directors of JapanCross, an electronic trading system for Japanese equities. He has served on the boards of BRUT and MarketXT, two electronic communications networks, as well as the managing advisory committee for Primex, an electronic auction facility of Nasdaq.

Before coming to Wall Street, Mr. Harts worked in the information technology industry for more than twelve years and is the developer of a best selling data communications software package. His articles on various aspects of the computer industry have been published internationally in PC Magazine.

Andrew Howieson is closely associated with State Street Corporation's electronic transaction initiatives in currency, equity and fixed-income markets. At the time of this conference, Andy headed a State Street subsidiary, Advance Auctions, provider of Bond Connect, an innovative market for fixed income trading. At State Street, Andy was successively responsible for Corporate Strategy & Business Development, SSIP (and incubator for re-trade and trade related business initiatives, and Advance Auctions. Prior to State Street, Andy had a successful career in operations and internal audit management with leading global banks and financial institutions.

Peter Jenkins is a Managing Director and Head of North American Equity Trading. Jenkins joined DeAM in 2002 when DeAM acquired Zurich Scudder Investments, where he served as Head of Global Equity Trading for 16 years. Prior to that, Jenkins spent three years as a senior trader at Cigna Investment Management. He began his career as a trader in 1980, working for three years as a trader at Zurich Scudder Investments.

Jenkins received a BS from the University of Connecticut. He is a member of the Investment Company Institute's Equity Market Task Force, the Institutional Traders Committee of the Security Traders Association, the New York Stock Exchange's Institutional Traders Advisory, the Trader Forum Advisory Board, and the National Organization of Investment Professionals.

In addition, Jenkins serves on the boards of W.R. Hambrecht & Co. and the James E. Olsen Memorial Foundation. Formerly, Jenkins served as the Chairman of the Securities Traders Association Institutional Committee (1977 and 1988) and served two consecutive terms as Chairman of Institutional Traders Advisory Committee at the New York Stock Exchange. He served as Vice Chairman for the NASDAQ/AMEX Institutional Organization of Investment Professionals in 1999 and served on the Board of Directors of the National Organization of Investment Professionals.

An active member of the industry, Jenkins was selected by Arthur Levitt, Chairman of the SEC, to participate in an industry panel on market transparency and was also selected to participate on a committee of representatives from the Investment Company Institute with SIA representatives to form a joint opinion on market transparency. He was chosen by William Lupien to provide input on a new electronic trading system called OptiMark and chaired the advisory committee on the issue. In addition, Jenkins led an industry group of buyside traders to gain direct access to Selectnet and worked on the Liquidnet advisory board to help establish the new ATS. He set up a new and improved Institutional Committee for the STA and became the second chairman of the committee. Jenkins has testified before the House Subcommittee on Finance on "The New Electronic Market" and the Subcommittee on Securities and Investment on the merits of decimalization.

In 1986, **Raymond Killian, Jr.** and a group of colleagues initiated plans for a computerized crossing network that ultimately became Investment Technology Group, a unit of Jefferies Group. In 1990, he assumed the full-time responsibility as Chief Executive Officer of ITG Inc., and he became Chairman of the Board in 1997. ITG has been a public company since 1994 and is listed on the New York Stock Exchange, symbol:ITG. The company's primary business is the development of technology to assist clients in controlling risk and cost in the equity execution process. ITG's products are considered cutting edge and the company has never had an unprofitable quarter since September 1988.

Mr. Killian was an Executive Vice President of Jefferies Group from 1985 to 1995, a Director and an Executive Vice President of Jefferies Group's wholly owned broker-dealer subsidiary, Jefferies & Company, Inc., from 1985 to 1991 and served as National Sales Manager of Jefferies from 1985 to 1990. He was a Director of Jefferies Group from January 1985 to 1999.

Mr. Killian was with Goldman Sachs from 1968 to 1985 and was Vice President and Manager of that firm's Institutional Sales from 1982 to 1985. He has been associated with The Cotting School for handicapped children in Lexington, Massachusetts for over forty years, and for the past fifteen, has served as Chairman of its Board of Trustees. Mr. Killian does fundraising for Cathedral High School Inner City Program of the Archdiocese of Boston. He is past Governor of the Boston Stock Exchange and has served on the Board of Directors for the National Organization of Investment Professionals. He has also testified before Congress on Markets 2000 issues and is a frequent speaker at investment technology conferences. He has been a guest lecturer at Harvard, MIT and Stanford Business schools.

Mr. Killian has a BS degree from Boston University. He resides in Manhattan and Rockport, Massachusetts with his first, and only, wife Helen and with whom he shares responsibility for five children, their spouses and nine grandchildren.

Jan Kregel is currently High Level Expert in International Finance serving in the New York office of the United Nations Conference on Trade and Development. He held the position of Senior Economic Advisor to the President of Confindustria, Guido Carli, from 1977-80; Advisor to the Secretary General of Economic Planning of the Ministry of the Budget, 1980-82, as well as participating in the Senior Management Training programs of IRI-Finmeccanica, Olivetti and Sinnea.

A Life Fellow of the Royal Economic Society (U.K.), an Elected member of the Società Italiana degli Economisti, and a member of the American Economic Association, biographical entries appear in all editions of Who's Who in Economics, and recent editions of Who's Who in Europe, and Who's Who in the World. Professor Kregel received his training in economics at Rutgers University in the US and the University of Cambridge in England; he has held permanent and visiting positions in universities in the Italy, United Kingdom, the United States, the Netherlands, Belgium, France, Germany and Mexico.

David Krell is a founder and President and Chief Executive Officer of the International Securities Exchange. From 1997 to 1998, he was Chairman and co-founder of K-Squared Research, LLC, a financial services consulting firm. From 1984 to 1997, Mr. Krell was Vice President, Options and Index Products, of the New York Stock Exchange where he managed marketing, systems and new product introductions for the division. From 1981 to 1984, Mr. Krell was First Vice President at the Chicago Board Options Exchange, responsible for the management and operation of the Marketing and Sales Division. Mr. Krell was also a Vice President of Merrill Lynch from 1978 to 1981 and founded its Managed Options Service.

Active in numerous industry groups, Mr. Krell is a Director on the Board of the International Federation of Technical Analysts, a former president of the Market Technicians Association and a past Director on the Board of The Options Clearing Corporation. As well, Mr. Krell was an Adjunct Professor at Rutgers University Graduate School of Management and at the Graduate School of Baruch College. He has also taught, coordinated and directed numerous seminars and workshops at the New York Institute of Finance. Mr. Krell holds an M.B.A. from Bernard Baruch College and a B.A. from Queens College.

William Lupien established OptiMark, Inc. in 1996, with an objective to improve the structure and operational capabilities of the securities market. Mr. Lupien is co-inventor of OptiMark's patented trading technology, a revolutionary method of structuring markets for securities and other fungible items.

Mr. Lupien has been active in the securities industry since joining the California-based brokerage firm of Mitchum, Jones & Templeton, Inc. (MJT), in 1965. Mr. Lupien served as chairman and CEO of MJT, while also a specialist on the floor of the Pacific Stock Exchange for 17 years. He was a Nasdaq market maker for 5 years. Upon leaving MJT in 1983, Mr. Lupien served as president, then chairman and CEO of Instinet Corporation, and was responsible for Instinet's move into trading Nasdaq stocks. During Mr. Lupien's tenure, Instinet's trading volumes increased tenfold, its revenues increased seventeen-fold, and the company was acquired by Reuters Plc.

In addition to his work within the securities industry, Mr. Lupien has served on numerous private and public company boards, including current positions on the boards of Ashton Technologies and St. Jude's Childrens Hospital. Mr. Lupien is a graduate of San Diego State University. His interests include horseback riding, fly fishing, photography, the history of the American West, music, travel, art, and gardening.

Duncan Niederauer became a Managing Director in 1997 and, in 2000, he relocated to the headquarters of Spear, Leeds & Kellogg, which Goldman Sachs acquired. In this capacity, he manages the Equities Division's direct access and electronic trading efforts, working closely with the division's product leaders. Previously, he ran the Equities E-Commerce effort, was the global head of portfolio trading, and spent three years in Tokyo in Derivatives and Japanese products. He joined the firm in 1985 and the equities division in 1987.

Duncan serves on the Firmwide Recruiting Committee, the Equities Division Technology Committee, the Colgate University Alumni Board of Directors and is a director of Eze Castle Software and Archipelago. He received an MBA from Emory University in 1985 and a BA from Colgate University in 1981.

Kenneth Pasternak is a co-founder of Knight Trading Group, Inc. He served as the Company's Chief Executive Officer from its founding in 1995 until his retirement on January 31, 2002 and as Chairman of Knight's Board of Directors from October 2000 until January 31, 2002.

Kenny co-founded Knight with Walter Raquet, Steve Steinman and Rob Lazarowitz in 1995 to provide self-directed individual investors with the same low cost, immediacy and dependability in their securities transactions enjoyed by institutional investors. Under Kenny's leadership, Knight became the leading wholesale market maker in the US securities markets, serving institutions in addition to broker-dealers, and expanding its presence into global markets in Japan and Europe.

Knight is the largest independent wholesale Nasdaq and non-Nasdaq OTC market maker, as well as the largest trading firm in the Nasdaq InterMarket, the electronic market for trading of exchange-listed securities, including those listed on the New York Stock Exchange (NYSE). In options trading, Knight is the fourth largest player with a significant presence on all five US options exchanges and in Europe. In addition, Knight manages an asset management business, Deephaven Capital Management, considered to be among the top three market neutral funds in the marketplace.

Prior to founding Knight, Kenny was a SVP, Limited Partner and Trading Room Manager for Spear, Leeds & Kellogg/Troster Singer, from 1979 until 1994. Kenny serves on the Board of Directors for Nasdaq, on the Advisory Committee of BRASS Utility, LLC (BRUT), and on the Board of Directors of Easdaq. He is often called upon to provide testimony to the US Congress regarding important market structure issues. Kenny received a B.A. from the State University of New York at New Paltz in 1976.

Junius Peake is Monfort Distinguished Professor of Finance at the University of Northern Colorado, where he has been a professor for 10 years. Prior to that time he was in the financial industry for more than 40 years, both as a senior officer of a large broker-dealer in New York, and as a domestic and international consultant. His consultancies have included assignments in the former Soviet Union and China, as well as Europe and South America.

Professor Peake's particular area of interest and expertise is financial market microstructure, which studies how markets are organized, governed and operated. He was the principal author of a seminal proposal on the use of computers in the trade entry, execution and reporting presented to the National Market Advisory Board of the Securities & Exchange Commission in 1976, and has been invited to speak at many industry conferences during the past 25 or more years. He is considered an international expert in the market microstructure field of academia.

In addition to his work on the use of computers in financial trading systems, he has also been called the "father of decimalization," in which the pricing of securities has recently changed from fractions to decimals, saving investors billions of dollars annually. In the early 1980s, Mr. Peake founded the International Futures Exchange (Bermuda) Ltd. ("INTEX"), where the first electronic futures trades were made.

Professor Peake was a former Governor and Vice-Chairman of the National Association of Securities Dealers, Inc., and has been a featured speaker at the Wharton School of the University of Pennsylvania, the Amos Tuck School of Dartmouth, Northwestern University, the University of Chicago, the University of Memphis, and the Leonard Stern School of New York University. He is quoted often in publications such as the Wall Street Journal, the Financial Times (London), Business Week, Forbes and US News and World Report. He has also appeared on national television business programs of CNN, CNBC, CBS and WWOR-TV.

Gerald (Jerry) Putnam is the founder and Chief Executive Officer of Archipelago Holdings, the parent company of the Archipelago Exchange and the Archipelago Electronics Communications Network (ECN). Jerry has attracted major investors to Archipelago from both the institutional and retail financial services sectors. Archipelago's leading-edge technology, open architecture and unbiased trading platform provide investors with fast, cost-efficient and anonymous market access. In March of 2002, trading began on the Archipelago Exchange, the nation's first totally open, all-electronic national stock exchange. The Archipelago ECN, one of four original ECNs, was formed in December 1996 with software developer Townsend Analytics. It contends for the greatest trading volume in Nasdaq stocks among all ECNs.

In January 2002, Jerry was inducted into the Entrepreneurship Hall of Fame sponsored by the University of Illinois at Chicago. Jerry was named one of Time Magazines Innovators in Finance in October 2000.

Jerry has developed a deep understanding of the securities industry through his involvement in institutional and derivative sales at several major brokerage firms in New York and Chicago since 1983.

He was at Walsh, Greenwood from 1983 to 1987, and moved to Chicago in 1985 to open their institutional sales desk. From there, he gained further experience at Jefferies & Company, Paine Webber, Prudential and Geldermann Securities, Inc.

Moving into the electronic trading arena in 1994, Jerry founded Terra Nova, an on-line broker-dealer, and was its president until January 1999. He currently serves on Terra Nova's Board of Directors.

Jerry received a Bachelor of Science degree in economics with a major in accounting from the University of Pennsylvania, Wharton School in 1981.

James Ross is Senior Vice President for Global Strategic Business and Sales (SBG) at Instinet Corporation. Since mid-2001, he has been building and overseeing a team of highly experienced and knowledgeable sales people who are responsible for globally and strategically orchestrating and prioritizing Instinet's many businesses, products, services and relationships for the top global banks, traditional asset managers and plan sponsors. The SBG team is also responsible for building senior management relationships with these firms in order to establish an atmosphere of partnership and collaboration. In addition to these duties, Mr. Ross is also on the board of the JapanCross and continues to champion the concept of call market trading. He is a frequent speaker at financial markets conferences regarding market structure, design and innovation.

From 1989 until 2001, Mr. Ross was Senior Vice President of Global Instinet Crossing, Instinet's after-hours equity trading product provides the opportunity to lower transaction costs by providing customers a passive trading environment. In this position, he was responsible for all Crossing business, sales and development, both international and domestic. During his tenure, he was responsible for the strategic joint venture with NSSB to establish the JapanCross Securities Company in Tokyo. JapanCross is the first off-exchange Japanese equity crossing system. In addition, Mr. Ross has championed call market trading issues and initiatives in the single-price auction and non-equity type environments like FX.

Mr. Ross joined Instinet as a Crossing Network Sales Assistant in 1989. He came to Instinet from the consulting firm Booz Allen & Hamilton, where he was Research Assistant, supporting the Department of the Navy. He has also spent time on Capital Hill, first as a Legislative Assistant in the Senate, then as a Field Representative in the House. Mr. Ross received his B.A. in English Literature with Honors from Bates College.

Instinet Corporation, member NASD/SIPC. JapanCross is an independent broker created by a 50:50 joint venture between Instinet International Corporation, a subsidiary of Instinet Group Incorporated or any of its US broker/dealer subsidiaries.

Robert A. Schwartz is Marvin M. Speiser Professor of Finance and University Distinguished Professor in the Zicklin School of Business, Baruch College, CUNY. Before joining the Baruch faculty in 1997, he was Professor of Finance and Economics and Yamaichi Faculty Fellow at New York University's Leonard N. Stern School of Business, where he had been a member of the faculty since 1965. Professor Schwartz received his Ph.D. in Economics from Columbia University. His research is in the area of financial economics, with a primary focus on the structure of securities markets. He has published numerous journal articles and seven books, including *Reshaping the Equity Markets: A Guide for the 1990s,* Harper Business, 1991 (reissued by Business One Irwin, 1993). He has served as a consultant to various market centers including the New York Stock Exchange, the American Stock Exchange, Nasdaq, the London Stock Exchange, Instinet, the Arizona Stock Exchange, Deutsche Börse, and the Bolsa Mexicana. From April 1983 to April 1988, he was an associate editor of *The Journal of Finance,* and he is currently an associate editor of the *Review of Quantitative Finance and Accounting,* the *Review of Pacific Basin Financial Markets and Policies,* and *The Journal of Entrepreneurial Finance & Business Ventures,* and is a member of the advisory board of *International Finance.* In December, 1995, Professor Schwartz was named the first chairman of Nasdaq's Economic Advisory Board, and he served on the EAB until Spring 1999.

Glen Shipway is the Chief Executive Officer of Primex Trading NA, a company formed in 1998 for the sole purpose of creating an electronic auction system for the trading of equities and options in the US. After two years of development, the Primex Auction system, which is operated by Nasdaq for their New York and Nasdaq listed equities trading, was launched in December 2001. For the 10 years prior to joining Primex Trading, Glen worked for The Nasdaq Stock Market. When he retired in 1999, he was the Executive Vice President for Market Services. From 1973 to 1989 he was head of equity, debt, option, and commodity trading at Interstate Securities, Charlotte NC, Glen entered the securities business in 1967 as an examiner with the NASD.

Cameron Smith is General Counsel of The Island ECN, Inc., the second-largest alternative trading system. In this position he is responsible for all legal and regulatory issues for Island, which recently announced plans to file with the SEC for stock exchange status.

Earlier in his career, Mr. Smith was dedicated to securities regulation, and served as an attorney in the SEC's Division of Market Regulation and later as senior counsel in the Office of Compliance Inspections and Examinations. In this capacity, he participated in several surveillance examinations of all nine national securities markets, including the New York Stock Exchange and Nasdaq. In addition to routine inspections, Mr. Smith performed special purpose examinations of broker-dealers and clearing corporations.

Prior to joining Island in 1998, Mr. Smith was a deputy project manager with The Intrados Group, a USA.I.D. capital markets project in Moldova. Mr. Smith assisted in the formulation of the business plan for the Moldova Stock Exchange and Broker-Dealer Association. He has also served as a consultant for Financial Markets International, a USA.I.D. capital markets development project in Romania, where he was connected with the successful opening of the Romanian over-the-counter market.

Mr. Smith earned a J.D. from Seattle University School of Law, where he graduated in the top third of his class, and holds a BA in Finance from the University of Washington. He is a member of the Washington State Bar Association.

The Island ECN, Inc. is an electronic order-matching system that gives brokerage firms the power to electronically display and match stock orders for retail and institutional investors. Island is a fair and impartial stock trading forum where buyers and sellers meet directly. Island's efficient and reliable system, each day transacting more than $5 billion in dollar volume, reduces costs to both brokerage firms and investors. The alternative trading pioneer, Island is located online at www.isld.com and is headquartered in New York City.

George Sofianos joined Goldman Sachs in January 2001 and he is leading the firm's trading costs and market structure research effort for equities. Prior to joining Goldman Sachs, he was Vice President and Head of Research at the New York Stock Exchange. In that capacity, he oversaw the development and maintenance of databases, the production of trading statistics, reports and research papers.

Before joining the NYSE, he worked at the Federal Reserve Bank of New York, in the Financial Studies department and at the Open Markets Desk. Prior to that, he spent three years teaching economics and finance at the Stern Graduate School of Business, New York University.

Mr. Sofianos has published research on trading costs, the cross listing and trading of non-US stocks, the NYSE specialist trading behavior, stock price behavior on expirations, the impact of program trading on intraday stock price volatility, index arbitrage, margin requirements, and monetary policy. He holds BSc and MSc. degrees from the London School of Economics and received his Ph.D. in economics from Harvard University.

Holly Stark is Principal and Director of Trading at Kern Capital Management. Holly manages Kern Capital Management's trading desk and is responsible for developing execution strategies designed to maximize returns while minimizing transaction costs. Prior to joining Kern Capital Management in 2000, Holly was with Dalton, Greiner, Hartman, Maher & Co. (DGHM) for ten years where she was responsible for all trading activities. For eight years prior to DGHM, Holly was with Dillon, Read Capital, Inc., the predecessor firm to DGHM. Through her current and past participation on advisory committees at the NASD, New York Stock Exchange and The Investment Company Institute, Holly is actively involved with the changing structure of today's capital markets. Holly earned her Bachelor of Arts from Rutgers College in 1978.

Benn Steil is the André Meyer Senior Fellow in International Economics at the Council on Foreign Relations in New York. He is also the Editor of *International Finance* (Blackwell Publishers); a co-founder and director of Efficient Frontiers Ltd, a markets consultancy; a non-executive director of the virt-x stock exchange in London; a member of the European Shadow Financial Regulatory Committee; and a member of the Advisory Board of the European Capital Markets Institute. Until November 1998, he was Director of the International Economics Program at the Royal Institute of International Affairs in London. Prior to his appointment at the Institute in 1992, he held a Lloyd's of London Tercentenary Research Fellowship at Nuffield College, Oxford, where he received his PhD in Economics.

Dr. Steil has written and spoken widely on securities trading and market regulation. His research and market commentary are regularly covered in publications such as the *Financial Times, Wall Street Journal, New York Times, International Herald Tribune, USA Today, The Economist, Barrons, Business Week, Fortune, Time, Newsweek, Securities Industry News, Financial News, Traders Magazine,* and Reuters and Bloomberg online. Among his books are a critically acclaimed study of *The European Equity Markets* and a major text on *Institutional Investors*, as well as edited volumes on cross-border antitrust (*Antitrust Goes Global*) and the economics of innovation (*Technological Innovation and Economic Performance*). His other areas of published research include derivatives, risk management, decision theory, and international trade. Dr. Steil has also worked for investment banks in New York and London, in systems analysis and foreign exchange, and currently provides consultancy services to exchanges, securities houses, government bodies and international organizations around the world.

Daniel Weaver is currently an Associate Professor of Finance in the Zicklin School of Business, Baruch College, CUNY. He has served on the faculty of Rutgers University, The American University, and Marquette University and holds degrees in English literature (BA, Seton Hall University) and finance (MBA, Ph.D. Rutgers University).

Dan's research and teaching focus is on security design, security market structure, and e-commerce. He has over 25 published articles. Recent papers include an examination of the value of specialists, the impact of anonymity on the quotation of Nasdaq market makers, the impact of the public disclosure of limit order books on liquidity, potential visibility gains as a reason for listing, and the impact of tick size on market quality. He has served as a consultant to the American Stock Exchange, New York Stock Exchange, Stockholm Stock Exchange, Toronto Stock Exchange, and the Securities Industry Association.

Dan has been widely quoted in newspapers across the country including the Wall Street Journal, New York Times, Washington Post, USA Today, Associated Press, Barron's, Securities Week, Traders, and the Los Angeles Times. He has appeared on CNN, CNBC, PBS, NPR, and local radio and television. He has testified before the House Commerce Committee on the subject of decimalization.

Bruce Weber is Associate Professor of Computer Information Systems and Director of the Subotnick Financial Services Center at the Zicklin School of Business, Baruch College, CUNY. He has an AB in Applied Mathematics from Harvard University, and M.A. and Ph.D. in Decision Sciences from the Wharton School of the University of Pennsylvania. His research examines the economic impact of next-generation financial technologies, and in particular, securities market trading mechanisms. His publications have appeared in a number of information systems and management science journals, and he is an editorial board member of Information Systems Research and Electronic Markets. He is co-developer, with Robert A. Schwartz, of the market trading model used for the NASD "HeadTrader" game, which is available at http://www.nasd.com/HeadTrader.

Robert Wood is a Distinguished Professor of Finance at the University of Memphis. Professor Wood previously taught at Penn State University for 14 years and NYU for one year. His education includes a PhD in Finance from the University of Pittsburgh, a Masters in Operations Research from Stanford University, and a Bachelor in Economics from the University of Washington. He was a member of the Presidential Task Force on Market Mechanisms (The Brady Commission) that studied the market crash in 1987, and a founding member of the NASD Economic Advisory Board. Professor Wood is the founder and Executive Director of the Institute for the Study of Security Markets, a nonprofit Educational Foundation that promotes securities markets research by providing transactions data to academic institutions. He has consulted for various stock exchanges and investment firms around the world. Prior to becoming an academic, Professor Wood held various positions in industry over a fifteen-year period.

Susan Woodward is the chairman and founder of Sand Hill Econometrics, a research and consulting firm specializing in venture capital, financial markets, and mortgage lending. She did both her BA and PhD in economics at UCLA. From 1975 to 1985, she taught finance and economics at UCLA and other major universities. From 1985 to 1995 she served in three senior positions in the Federal government. First, she served as senior staff economist for financial markets and institutions at the Council of Economic Advisors; second, she served as chief economist and Deputy Assistant Secretary at the US Department of Housing and Urban Development; and third, she served as chief economist at the US Securities and Exchange Commission. A native and homesick Californian, in 1995 she returned to California. From 1998-2001 she was on the senior management team for OffRoad Capital, an on-line investment bank, and was principle designer of an electronic auction system to fund venture companies on the internet. With the expertise in venture financing gained at OffRoad, she founded Sand Hill Econometrics to develop and market an index of value for venture capital. She currently resides in Menlo Park.

R. Steven Wunsch is President of AZX, Inc., a company formed to design, build, market and operate an electronic single price auction trading system. Previously, Mr. Wunsch worked in the Financial Futures Department of Kidder, Peabody, where he was a Vice President responsible for the Department's institutional customer index futures and equity trading activities. Prior to joining Kidder, Peabody, he was a floor trader and broker on the Amex Commodities and New York Futures Exchanges. Mr. Wunsch received a B. A. in English Literature in 1969 from Princeton University.

INDEX

Note: The use of *n* or *nn* following a page number refers to a particular footnote or range of footnotes on that page.

Lightning Source UK Ltd.
Milton Keynes UK
15 January 2010

148660UK00007B/20/A

9 780792 374237